JUSTICE

OR

JUST US

Resist.
Redeem.
Reclaim.
Renew.

by
Jaime M. Kowlessar

Justice or Just Us
Published by
Watersprings Media House, LLC.
P.O. Box 1284
Olive Branch, MS 38654
For bulk orders or permission requests contact publisher. www.waterspringsmedia.com

Copyright © 2018, 2019 by Jaime M. Kowlessar. All rights reserved.

No part of this book may be reproduced in any form or by any electronic or mechanical means, including information storage and retrieval systems, without written permission from the author, except for the use of brief quotations in a book review.

ISBN 13: 978-1-948877-20-6

Table of Contents

INTRODUCTION 4

1/ I STILL CAN'T BREATHE 5

2/ DO THE RIGHT THING 20

3/ DON'T HATE THE PLAYA HATE THE GAME 28

4/ STAY WOKE!!! 45

5/ THIS IS MY STORY...63

6/ DANCING WITH THE SCARS.............................80

7/ CRISIS IN THE VILLAGE 102

8/ HOW TO GET AWAY WITH MURDER? 127

9/ WHY WE CAN'T BE SILENT 151

10/ JESUS, THE TROUBLE MAKER 172

11/ WITH LIBERTY AND JUSTICE, FOR JUST US...192

ABOUT THE AUTHOR 211

Introduction

This book is a compilation of sermons that I've written over the years on the topic of social justice. I hope that these words will inspire you to resist the empire, redeem the oppressed, reclaim them as our own, and renew them from their old state to a better version of themselves.

At the end of each chapter, there are questions for you to reflect on by yourself or with a group and a prayer. The sermons in this book are in most cases in the same language that was used to when I preached them at various churches.

P.S. I ask of you only one favor, that when you are finished, please share this book with someone who you think would benefit from it.

Resist
Redeem
Reclaim
Renew

1

I Still Can't Breathe

Exodus 6:10-13
Therefore, say to the people of Israel: 'I am the Lord, I will free you from your oppression and will rescue you from your slavery in Egypt. I will redeem you with a powerful arm and great acts of judgement. I will claim you as my own people, and I will be your God. Then you will know that I am the Lord your God who has freed you from your oppression in Egypt. I will bring you into the land I swore to give to Abraham, Isaac, and Jacob. I will give it to you as your very own possession. I am the Lord. So Moses told the people of Israel what the Lord had said, but they refused to listen anymore. They had become too discouraged by the brutality of their slavery. "And the Lord spake unto Moses, saying, Go in, speak unto Pharaoh king of Egypt, that he let the children of Israel go out of his land. And Moses spake before the Lord, saying, Behold, the children of Israel have not hearkened unto me; how then shall Pharaoh hear me, who am of uncircumcised lips? And the Lord spake unto Moses and unto Aaron, and gave them a charge unto the children of Israel, and unto Pharaoh king of Egypt, to bring the children of Israel out of the land of Egypt."

I think I'll start by taking a page out of the book of Lil Wayne this morning. Wayne so eloquently said, "I could mingle with the stars, and throw a party on Mars, I am a prisoner locked up behind Xanax Bars". Deep down I guess Wayne is describing what most of us feel from day to day. You don't have to be in prison to feel like a prisoner. You could be the life of the party, but you are miserable inside. You could feel like you are on top of the world but go to sleep with the world on top of you. You could have all the words to say to everyone else, but nothing to say to yourself. On the outside, you could look like you got it going on, but deep down inside you are a hot mess.

Life has a way of taking everything good and turning it around for the worse. Live long enough and sooner or later you are going to have some good days, and some bad days. One day you could feel like you are winning only to realize that you are still 20 points down in the 4th quarter of life.

As long as I stay black, I'll never forget this. Last Christmas I bought my daughters a board game. I played a few games with them, after a while I left them to go do something else. A few minutes after I left, I heard my youngest daughter Amber crying. She comes into eh room and say, baby, what's wrong. With tears in her eyes...she Daddy, whenever I'm about to win the game Katelynn always changes the rules.

Ain't it safe to say, that's what life is like most people. Every time it feels like we gon' win they are always trying to change the rules. The injustice of our justice system continues to fail its citizens. Agent Orange, Adolf Twitler, Vanilla Isis, The Cheeto in Chief, Lying King, aka #45, aka He that was sent to sent to destroy and divide America, ignored Puerto Rico, still wants to build a wall, end DACA. The same person that wasted no time to call his own citizens terrorist, but if you are white and shoot 18 people we need more time to think about it. Is it me, or am I the only that is suffering from the effects of Executive Disorder. Ain't it crazy how we have watched decency, diplomacy, and dignity walk out of the white house and now we've got disorder, dereliction, and disrespect. It's not just Agent Orange, but it's also his Trumpets.

Since you guys are bible scholars you understand the context of the text. Pharaoh is in power. The bible says that it's a new Pharaoh, one who did not know Joseph. I wish I could tell you how this Pharaoh got in power but I don't. Perhaps he had meetings with the Russiannites, and they took out ads on Egyptian social media and told him that we have telegrams from your opponent. Maybe he won the electoral college, but we know it wasn't the popular vote. Nevertheless, he is in power.

Not only is he in power but Israelites are victims of his harsh and cruel regime. Policies and laws that favor the have-gots and ignore the have-nots. For 200 years the children of Israel were enslaved in Egypt. Trapped by their oppressor. Hard pressed with their backs up against the wall. They've gotta make bricks without straw. Exodus 1:12 says, that the more they persecuted them, the more they multiplied.

I don't know about you, but I know growing up in America life has pushed our backs up against the wall but, it was that struggle that made us stronger. We learned how to make a way out of no way. I remember when we didn't have any more toothpaste. We didn't go to store and buy a new one, but we bent that top, squeezed that thing, then roll that thing, and you had about a month more of toothpaste. When we ran out of lotion, we used to turn that thing upside down, then you cut that top off of that thing. We didn't buy a new TV when we didn't get the channel; we found an old wire hanger, when the knob fell off you got a pair of pliers out of the closet. In these still waiting to be United States of America we've been making bricks without straw, because there is a strength inside of us that won't let us give up.

Our scripture today tells us that Moses comes to Israel with a word from God. He says, "This is It". The God of Abraham, Isaac, and Jacob, has told me that your deliverance is on its way. Today we break free from the bondage of our oppressors.

Verse 9 is strange the text says, "But they refused to listen anymore. They had become too discouraged by the brutality of their slavery." According to Rabbi

Sharon Brous she says that A better translation of the text would be they could not hear him because of shortness or anguish of breath and hard work.

They could not breathe. When the realities of this world rock us from left to right, any news we get can sound like bad news. Just like the children of Israel we are out of breath. When you are out of breath, it is impossible to process or think about your next move. No matter what we do, every step forward seems like two steps backwards. I'm feeling Sis. Fannie Lou Hamer, I'm sick and tired of being sick and tired.

I still can't breathe. I was reading the book Chokehold by Paul Butler, and in that book, Mr. Butler uses as analogy the chokehold to describe what life is like for Black and Brown Americans. When the officers used the chokehold on Eric Garner, although it was illegal, they were trying to get him to comply, but he could not why because he could not breathe. Paul Butler says that the American justice system is like a vice grip for poor people just trying to breathe. The unjust justice system in America. In America, you have to realize that just because it's the law, it doesn't make it just. My favorite preacher Dr. Frederick D. Haynes says,

Slavery was legal, but it was not just.
Jim Crow was legal, but it was not just.
Segregation was legal, but it was not just.
3 strikes was legal, but it was not just.
Cash bail bonds system making poor people pay for freedom is legal, but it ain't just.
It was legal to kill Jesus, but it was not just.

Yeah, we got laws but not every law is just. And it can feel like you are in a chokehold. We see the hurricanes, the floods, and fires which is evidence of climate control and not something created by the Chinese.

We know that black and brown folks across the country are criminalized, racially profiled, and ostracized by society, whilst white nationalists have free access to the white house.

We see the continued false narratives that have been aimed at the Muslim community that tries to label all of them as terrorist …we can't even tell the difference between a Suni and Shiite, but as long as they where a towel on their head, they must be a threat to our national security.

We see the spike in anti-semitism and hate crimes against vulnerable minority communities.

We lay witness to the racial profiling of the Mexican immigrants whose country we stole from them in the first place, and as our nation tries to strips them of their God-given right to have access equality and opportunities.

We see the continued and deepened efforts to undermine health care for those that need it the most. And now a tax bill reform that appears to take from needy and give to the greedy.

We see the continued predatory harassment and violence against women primarily African American women by shaming them through their hair and features. Unequal pay as well as the continued pressure and intimidation towards LGBTQ community that transcends beyond whatever party you support.

We see the church has abandoned the struggle, instead of being on the frontlines in the fight for civil liberties, we have thrown in the towel righteousness for political expediency and complicity. What has happened to the black church. Our theology has been hijacked by gospel pimping preachers of prosperity. We have subjugated God to a genie in the bottle that we just rub when want a blessing. We have surrendered church to solicit emotional fanfare, instead of intellectual stimulation. We care more about evoking feelings, and how high you jump instead of how straight you walk. We have stopped giving our members things to think about we just leave them feeling good. We've abandoned black theology for wack theology. Slaves obey your master theological discourse that creates a passive, inactive, docile member. Our church continues to promote propaganda by printing an image of a white supremacist version of Jesus that is theologically, geographically, and historically incorrect.

Our meetings are always revolving around more tithe, rather than more time saving and restoring humanity. Our churches are in neighborhoods that are consumed with crime, dropout factories, and payday loan advance shops. We have Grade A churches, with Grade A worship, and Grade A lunches, in Grade F neighborhoods, with failing schools and hungry children wondering where their next meal will come from. I stop by here to tell you that it's time that we put the neighbor back in the hood. When we abdicate our social responsibility to humanity, we abandon our duty as Christians. If the community is doing bad then the church is doing bad, because the Lord Told Jeremiah to pray for the peace of Babylon, that their prosperity will result in your prosperity.

The gospel and justice go hand in hand…Jesus read from the book of Isaiah in the temple on the Sabbath day…The spirit of the Lord is upon me…to bring good news to the poor, heal the brokenhearted, preach deliverance to the captives, give sight to the blind, and give liberty to the bruised. Then he says preach the acceptable year of the Lord…in other words the jubilee. In Duet. God says Remember the Sabbath because you were once slaves in Egypt. Therefore, if you were once a slave, then it's your responsibility to free others. Pay it forward.

Harriett Tubman has to be one of my favorite African heroes. When they asked Harriett why do you keep going back saving slaves. She said, "I ain't free until all my people are free."

Verse 10, says…Then the Lord spoke to Moses, go back to Pharaoh. I love that word Go, because it's action. I had a lively discussion with one of my colleagues in ministry about Activity versus Action. Activity is sitting in seminars and doing workshops, but Action is engaging in overturning systematic injustice. God says go back to Pharaoh and tell him to let my people go. Notice that Moses was not told to ask Pharaoh can you give us weekends off, can you we only work from 9-5, maybe some holidays. The message to Moses from God was specific and clear. It's freedom or nothing else. If we expect to create change, then our message must be specific, clear and concise.

The rest of the sentence God says to Moses, "Go back to Egypt", There are moments in your walk in Justice when you gotta go to hostile places. Yeah you gotta have courage. What is courage? Courage is a choice. Fear is a reaction, but Courage is a decision. Courage doesn't mean you don't get afraid; courage means you don't let fear stop you. You gonna lose some friends. You gonna love some family members. You may not get invited to go to certain places. You may have to do some things by yourself but know that not everything that you lose is a loss, but you gotta lose some things in order to get something better.

Moses continues to shoot back at God. Moses is like hey Israel won't listen to me, what makes you think that Pharaoh will listen to me. Moses said I'm a man of uncircumcised lips. In other words, I have clumsy speech. I'm tongue tied, and I stutter. I know this isn't part of the text, but Moses and God have this conversation before. God tells Moses you tell them I

Am that I am. I'm so glad that God did that...Could you imagine if God told him to say, I am the god of Abraham Isaac and Jacob, he who created the sun moon and stars...Moses would've messed up. But God said tell them I am that I am

I am water when you're thirsty

I am bread when you're hungry

I am light in the darkness

I am shelter in the storm

I am everything and anything I want to be...In short Moses, I am none of your business.

Stop thinking that you are not smart enough or strong enough to do social justice. God doesn't call people based on their strengths he calls you because you can be used. God doesn't call the qualified, but he qualifies the called. Not only does he qualify you, but he gives you what you need. The text tells us that God gives him Aaron.

We are called to extension chords of his power. What does an extension chord do? It takes power from one source and empowers another source. It's a hookup! God expects us to use our power to help others.

I won't forget the story of the little boy who was on the elevator with his father. As the doors of the elevator were closing the son asked the father would it be okay, if I held the door open for that man. The father gave the son permission to stand between the elevator doors to hold it open. When the man got on the elevator, he asked the little boy why would you do this for me? The little boy said, since we were going to the top, I figured that we might as well take somebody with us. Friends of mine if we are going to the top, lets make sure that we take somebody with us.

Take immigrants to the top

Take the community to the top

Take the brother on drugs to the top

Take the sister who has to sell her body to the top

Take thousands of children that go to be hungry to the top

Take our Muslim brothers to the top

Don't stop, until we all make it to the top!!!!

Reflections

- What are ways that we can change the narrative?
- What do you think about the current status of the church and its place in the community?
- Sometimes we think that a position means power, how can you use power given to you by God to influence and promote a change?

PRAYER

Father, I thank you, and I know that all power belongs to you, and through you, I can face all things. Help me Lord, to be the best version of me, so that our society can breathe by removing the chokehold.

AMEN

2

Do the Right Thing

Galatians 6:9-10

So let's not allow ourselves to get fatigued doing good. At the right time we will harvest a good crop if we don't give up, or quit. Right now, therefore, every time we get the chance, let us work for the benefit of all, starting with the people closest to us in the community of faith.

If you are like me, then you grew up in what was known as the golden age of Hip Hop. It was hard hitting beats, with meaningful lyrics. It was break dancing, popping and locking. Hip Hop was characterized by diversity, quality, innovation, and influence. Hip Hop in its purest form was born out of poverty and pain. It was revolutionary rhetoric, that spoke truth to power. It's not what we have today. It's not the shuck and jive minstrel show. Hip Hop was so powerful that VH1 didn't want to put their hands on it. MTV didn't want to look at it. Radio stations didn't want to put it on rotation. It was, *"Don't Push Me, Cuz I'm Close to the Edge, I'm trying not to lose my head…It's like a jungle sometimes it makes me wonder how I keep from going under".*

It was, *"Self Destruction, you're heading for self-destruction"…I never had to run from the Klu Klux Klan and shouldn't have to run from a black man."*

It was, *"Oooh Ladies first, Ladies First"…La Di Dadi we likes to party, we don't cause trouble and we don't bother nobody".*

I could go on for days, reminiscing about the songs that raised me, but if there was a group that stood out to me, and a monumental moment in my life, had to be 1989 and the song was called "Fight the Power", the song accompanied the movie "Do The Right Thing" directed by none other than Mr. Spike Lee himself.
Chuck D says,
"What we need is awareness / We can't get careless […] Let's get down to business / Mental self-defensive fitness"…We gotta Fight the Powers that Be.

Why, because Mr. Chuck D actualizes and realizes that there is a power, a system, a machine that's only desire is to pillage, and enslave communities. When the movie was released, and Chuck D wrote the song in the 80's, that decade represented a time of regression in the United States as it relates to racial equity similar to the time of the 1880s and the following decades when racial inequality was re-established following the Civil War and Reconstruction. The war on drugs that specifically targeted black and brown people. Economic policies that put millions of Americans out of jobs.

Shamefully and Sadly, the more things change, the more they stay the same. The lingering effects have Reaganism are still here, and now we have to deal with Trumponiaism. A president who has inspired and empowered right-wing 'so called'Christians to come out of the closet and justify his shameful policies and rhetoric. Even down to the state of Texas, a state that is so rich in wealth, and natural resources but yet has communities that are comparable to third world countries. Prison pipelines also known as your local high school.

Then to see a move of cowardice by Governor Greg Abbot of Texas, to sign Senate Bill 4 on a live stream event on a Sunday afternoon to put into effect a bill that will promote racial profiling and discrimination. A bill that will have many hard-working individuals afraid to come out of their homes. A bill that is antithetical to the biblical mandate which admonishes us to, welcome the stranger that is amongst us…

Then there is government sponsored terrorism with the shooting of Jordan Edwards. An unarmed 15-year-old murdered while leaving a party. Killed with no justification. To only have the officer lie in his report, and claim self-defense. To have a bond so low that it was paid immediately and he is released, whilst a mother must mourn rather than celebrate on mothers days.

These are just tips of the icebergs of the criminalization of the weak, and vulnerable of our society. The word of God says in Exodus 2:23, *years passed, and the king of Egypt died. but the Israelites continued to groan under their burden of slavery. They cried out of help, and their cry rose up to God."*

Because God heard their cry, the Lord raised up a brother, as a matter of fact, his name is Moses...His name means drawn out. God drew him out and turned the tables. He left the palace to come to the hood. *God says, in Exodus 3:7 "I have certainly seen the oppression of my people in Egypt. I have heard their cries of distress because of their harsh slave drivers. Yes I am aware of their sufferings."*

God hears the cries of humanity. Although their tears are not simply in the form of water running down their cheeks, but their tears and anger are manifesting itself in various forms. Violence, rioting, marching, depression, anger, these are their tears...but thanks be to God that he hears, and as the text states he is drawing us out to be the Moses of today. There is a work for us to do. When God sent Moses to Pharaoh there was no compromise, there were no negotiations, but Moses clearly expressed to Pharaoh that your system of injustice must be overturned and abolished.

As big and elaborate it was, God still used one man to shake the foundations of Egypt.

I can remember as a child I didn't have many toys, but there was one toy, in particular, that was called 'etch-a-sketch'. It was red, with two white knobs, and a screen. The one that is holding the soy would be able to use the two white knobs to sketch a picture, but here's the catch. Drawing with two white knobs wasn't easy, and sometimes you would create a mess, but the only way to clean the mess you would have to shake the etch-a-sketch and the mess that was made would get clean.

There is a mess in our world, and it's up to us to shake the foundations. Shake the foundation of this state to live up to the ideal of the constitution. Shake the foundations of a police system that is rooted in the slave watch program. Shake the foundations that create Islamophobia. Shake the foundations of bills that specifically target people and not policies.

I believe that God is calling us to do the Right Thing. God is calling us to fight the powers that be. God always raises up a leader to combat injustice. For every Pharaoh, there is a Moses. Forever fiery furnace, there are three Hebrew Boys. For every Nebuchadnezzar, there is a Daniel. For every Haman, there is an Esther. For every Agrippa, there is a Paul, and for every system of injustice that threatens the humanity, there is a YOU. God is calling you.

As the text says, So let's not allow ourselves to get fatigued doing good. At the right time, we will harvest a good crop if we don't give up, or quit. Right now, therefore, every time we get the chance, let us work for the benefit of all, starting with the people closest to us in the community of faith.

Reflections

Sometimes doing the right thing can make us feel very tired and fatigued. It's so much easier at times to just go along with the crowd and do what everyone else is doing. God never called us to fit in, but His desire is that we stand out. When we stand out, we actually stand up for those who can't do it for themselves. Today it is very important that you pray for the strength to do the right thing.

PRAYER

Lord, I thank you for the strength You have given to me make a difference. Please equip me with the tools that You already have so that I may have the courage to do the right thing.

AMEN

3

Don't Hate the Playa Hate the Game

Mark 2:23-27

One Sabbath day as Jesus was walking through some grainfields, his disciples began breaking off heads of grain to eat. But the Pharisees said to Jesus, "Look, why are they breaking the law by harvesting grain on the Sabbath?" Jesus said to them, "Haven't you ever read in the Scriptures what David did when he and his companions were hungry? He went into the house of God (during the days when Abiathar was high priest) and broke the law by eating the sacred loaves of bread that only the priests are allowed to eat. He also gave some to his companions." Then Jesus said to them, "The Sabbath was made to meet the needs of people, and not people to meet the requirements of the Sabbath. So the Son of Man is Lord, even over the Sabbath!"

Aren't you tired of games that people play? I mean, the reality is there will always be people that will try to play games with you. Truth be told it can make you sick and tired when you try to take yourself seriously, and folks always wanna mess with you. No matter who you are, you will find yourself in somebody's games. There was an old song, some of you might be too young to remember it, but the chorus went something like this, "Games people play, Night or day, they're just not matching what they should do...Keep me feeling blue"

Folks will try define you, and by defining you, they confine you to fit into their own little box.

There are games played on different levels; there are relationship games. Before you got together, it was cool. It was nice. You thought he or she was the best thing since crushed ice, but later on, you found out that you were dating an actor or an actress. You should've game them an Emmy, or an Oscar award, for all that drama they brought into your life.

There are victim games...Then there are those folks that will always make you feel bad because you could not be there. These 'those kind of folks' that think there is something wrong with other people, but they never see what's wrong with themselves. They will always call you and give you a ticket so you could ride with them on their guilt trip. Yeah, they put you on a guilt trip. Why you didn't call me? Why you didn't visit me? Why didn't you come pick me up? Excuse me, but I'm not trying to get contaminated by your Victim Thinking, because I got Victory Thinking.

Then there are games that are played in society. Every time it seems like we are getting close to knowing the rules, somebody changes the game. Every time you show up at your job, and you think you are making progress, somebody changes the game. Whenever you get to the table, and you're ready to order, somebody changes the menu. Oh, Y'all missing this...

Every time you try to sign up for free health care, all of a sudden the server is down. Every time you try to show up to vote, now you gotta have a voter registration card, and you woke up to realize that the place that you used to vote at, has now been moved to a new location.

Games y'all Games Games...Games people play, Night or day, they're just not matching what they should do...Keep me feeling blue"

In our text today, Jesus finds himself in a game. In a game that he did not create, originate, or initiate, but instead, he has become a player in this sick twisted scheme.

Mark introduces us to Jesus' social campaign. It is a campaign of action, and an assault on the Jewish Social Order in Capernaum. After he is baptized, Jesus begins to work. I like that; often times we wait too long before we start putting folk to work in the house of God. Here Jesus shows us, that it not just about baptizing folk, but it's also about empowering folk to be the best that they can be in doing the work of God.

Mark shows Jesus in Action. He is not dormant or dead; He is moving, and active. In chapter 1:21-28, Jesus casts out a demon. Next scene, Jesus heals Peter's mother in law, then in verse 32, the word says that evening after sunset, many sick and demon-possessed people were brought to Jesus. So, Jesus healed many people who were sick with various diseases, and he cast out many demons. Then in verse 35, he preaches in Galilee, goes into the town, and He heals a man with leprosy and tells him to go to the synagogue. Then in chapter 2, Jesus heals a paralyzed man, after he heals and forgives him, Jesus empowers him and tells him to pick up his bed and walk.

Jesus is changing the game. The rules of the Pharisees made it legal ostracize and marginalize the poor because they were sick. If they were sick, they could not work, and since they couldn't work, they didn't have money, and if you had no money, you could not purchase sacrifices to have your sins forgiven. To be cut off from the temple was to essentially say you are not a citizen, you are not a human being. You were a prisoner of society. By Jesus healing and delivering them he is doing a direct assault on the social order and caste system. Now those that were sick and cut off were grafted back into society as citizens.

In vs. 22, Jesus gives the people his campaign slogan, New wine calls for New wineskins.

Out with the old, and in with the new. This is a new society and a new world with new people new trends

Come thou font is a beautiful him, probably my favorite. That hymn can be distributed on many different mediums. You can put it on an 8 track, CD, or MP3, and the song will not change. The only problem with the 8 track (and in some cases CD's) is that if you give that to someone today, they would not know what to do with it. I find all too often that we are trying to do 8 track ministry for an MP3 generation.

Jesus is basically trying to remind us that you can't keep putting new wine in old wineskins. The content of our message doesn't have to change, but the methods by which we use to communicate them need to be revisited.

But as we look at the text, we discover that the Pharisees aren't on the same team. They are still playing their game. Mark, tells us that Jesus and his boys are walking through some grainfields on the Sabbath day. As they are walking through the grain fields, they are breaking off heads of grain to eat.

The Pharisees say, why are they breaking the law by harvesting grain on the Sabbath? I've noticed that there are always people that will always try to find fault in everything that you do. You always got folk that's going to nitpick and criticizes you whenever you don't do what they expect you to do. I mean all day, Jesus has been healing and delivering folk, now that he is walking through the grain field, and his boys are picking grain, they find fault with that.

Jesus proceeds to answer their foolish question, by taking them back to the book of Samuel. He begins his rebuttal by saying, Haven't you ever read…Haven't you ever studied? In other words, it's like Jesus saying if you don't know nothing don't say anything. You always find that it's them folk that think they know everything that always got something to say. Jesus says, haven't you ever read about what David did when he has friends were hungry? They went into the temple and ate the sacred loaves of bread.

So why are you mad, why are you pointing the finger? Why are you hating? I'm only doing what has been done before. Don't hate the player, hate the game. I had to look up what exactly does that phrase.

Don't hate the play means, and the urban dictionary helped me a lot.

Do not fault the successful participant in a flawed system; try instead to discern and rebuke that aspect of its organization which allows or encourages the behavior that has provoked your displeasure.

Don't dislike someone for their actions, consider instead the situation that causes it.

Jesus is saying I'm only doing what your ancestors have done. I'm only mimicking what I've seen, and what I know. My boys are hungry, and they need food to eat. I refuse to let them starve.

Instead of Jesus stopping them, he encourages them to continue eating. Don't ever let what people say about dictate what you do. TI said, "Never mind what haters say, ignore em till the fade away." Don't ever waste your time giving major energy to minor people. They hate you for the fact that you are showing them up. They are just mad that they can't do what you do so they make up things about you. After all, a hater man marries a hater woman, and they have hater kids.

Jesus didn't waste any time in meaningless rhetoric and discussion. I ain't got no time to argue with you, if you wanna be ignant then go on and be ignant, that's yo problem. Never stoop down or better yet. Don't live down to people's expectations.

But Jesus is also showing and revealing to us more about the game. The Pharisees are not simply mad that Jesus is doing this on the Sabbath, but their indignation with Jesus is the fact they are eating the grain. They are trampling on the grain. Jesus and the disciples are destroying and eating the grain. They are destroying and eating the product. They are destroying and eating their profits. He is messing with their money. He is messing with their investments. He is touching their supply.

History informs us that the Pharisees advocated local distribution, to ensure that provincial priests received their due of the grain. So, there was a lot of politics and money involved in the grain. There was a lobbying in the political arena for those who grew the grain, and what was done with the grain. Let me tell you once you start messing with folks money watch them come after you.

Jesus uses the story of David and his companions. Now when David and his companions went into the temple to eat the bread, it was not a Sabbath day. But Jesus uses the story to remind the Pharisees that David and his companions were on a mission and because they were on a mission they were hungry.

In 1 Samuel 21, David says the King has sent me on a mission. Because the King has sent me on a mission, I have authority to eat this bread, as well as my companions because we have a job to do. Jesus refers to that story, because the King (The Father) has sent Jesus on a mission, and that mission is to redeem the world, and right now in order to have strength I will use my authority to do that which I please because I am the HNIC...The Head Nazarene In Charge. I will engage in civil disobedience because a change has got to come. As a matter of fact, I hate the game, because you Pharisees are saying that the rules of the Sabbath should cause a person to go hungry instead of life.

The text invites us into the world of Jesus. Jesus hates the game, because economic distribution, and a lack of sharing the wealth. The good only went to the greedy and not to the needy.

Hate the game, that says because you live in a poor community you have to be subjected to a subpar educational system.

Hate the game, that still profiles black and brown boys.

Hate the game, that still makes our beautiful black and Hispanic women look like uneducated gold diggers.

Hate the game, that wants to already vilify those innocent children that are crossing the border to come to America

Jesus says, don't hate the player, hate the game. If you knew why we were picking grain, then you wouldn't be pointing the finger at us right now.

If you would understand why we picking food, then you would not judge. If you knew my options, then you wouldn't judge my choices. If you would understand why some people praise the way they do it's because you don't know what they've been through. There is always a story behind my glory.

The disciples were picking grain and eating because it was accessible to them. It was available to them. Understand that Jesus and disciples were traveling from town to town, and sometimes they would travel through deserts. The scarcity of food was enormous, so in a real sense, there were food deserts. By seeing the grain field, they took time to eat all they can at the buffet.

Have you ever noticed how you could drive in some areas and never see a whole foods, central market, sprouts, or Trader Joes? Have you ever noticed that healthy choices are inaccessible to people in low income areas?

Studies have found that wealthy districts have three times as many supermarkets as poor ones do, that white neighborhood contain an average of four times as many supermarkets as predominantly black ones do, and that grocery stores in African-American communities are usually smaller with less selection. People's choices about what to eat are severely limited by the options available to them and what they can afford—and many food deserts contain an overabundance of fast food chains selling cheap "meat" and dairy-based foods that are high in fat, sugar, and salt.

My state Texas has the largest "grocery gap" in the nation, which means it has a lower number of supermarkets per capita than any other state. This shortage of supermarkets creates very real barriers to access to healthy foods, particularly for lower-income Texans. Big chain supermarkets look at the education level of a community and determine where they will build their supermarkets.

All I'm saying is, don't just look to the have gots, you must remember the have-nots. We don't only wanna eat McDonalds, Fried Chicken, Ribs, and Liquor. We want Jamba Juice; we want some apples, cherries, and pineapples. We want free samples of good fruit. We eat mangos too. We eat wheat bread too. We would love to know the benefits of eating flax seed. We are willing to try sweet potato fries.

Jesus then informs them about the Sabbath. He says that the Sabbath was made to meet the needs of the people, and not people to meet the requirements of the Sabbath.

The text informs us that there is the Lord's Sabbath, and Man's Sabbath. There is Sabbath that was instituted at creation and reinstated at Sinai. Then there is a Sabbath created by man. The man-made Sabbath is full of rules and regulations. The man-made sabbath is a day that we hide behind our own religiosity and shelter ourselves from those that are in need. It's a man-made sabbath that only wants to study amongst yourself, and not try to study with others. For some of us we cover up our fear of reaching people by only coming here and going straight home until the sunsets and do what I got to do. Now there is nothing wrong with eating lunch, and studying on the Sabbath don't get it twisted...I do think that there is something wrong when you are so insulated and insular that when the opportunity arises to help, you choose yourself over those that are in need

What kind of sabbath do you keep...do you keep a self-serving sabbath or do you keep a serving Sabbath.

I'll never forget one day when I was at school, I couldn't get on the internet to do my work. Turns out that when I inquired about the problem, the IT guy told me that the servers were down. I said the servers are down?!? He said 'servers' are what keep the computers going, the internet running, and the printers printing. If the servers are down, then no work can be done.

And all I'm saying is that when the servers are down in the church, then the works stops flowing. The hungry will stay hungry. The homeless will stay homeless. The downtrodden will stay down. The hurt will always be bruised. The wanderer will never come back home.

Therefore, in the text, Jesus is showing the Pharisees, I ain't got no time for you, or for what you say, but because I'm God in the flesh. I am He that made all things. I've come so that I could serve others. "For the Son of man came not to be served, but to be a servant to all people.

And because Jesus is a servant I wanna be a co-laborer with glory.

If I can help somebody, as I pass along,
If I can cheer somebody, with a word or song,
If I can show somebody, how they're traveling wrong,
Then my living shall not be in vain

As a matter of fact, the greatest act of service is to sacrifice one's self for the sake of others.

Reflections

- Jesus said you can't put new wine, in old wineskins, in other words it's time for a change. What ways can you see the church trying to use old wine, to reach new people?
- Food deserts have always been a problem in poor communities. What are some practical ways we can address this growing and pervasive problem?
- What's the difference between the Lord's Sabbath and Man's Sabbath, and which one have you been observing?

PRAYER

Father, please make me a servant to all people. A servant that will show forth your praise. Help me to use the advantages that You've given to me help the disadvantaged. Thank you for your love.

AMEN

4

Stay Woke!!!

1 Chronicles 12:32

Of Issachar, those who had understanding of the times, to know what Israel ought to do, two hundred chiefs, and all their kindred under their command.

In case you've been living under a rock for the last few weeks, you would know that we are living in some terrible and turbulent times. As the days go on, it seems like it's getting worse and worse. God's word is fulfilling itself, as men's hearts are waxing colder than it has never been before.

The times are telling us and showing us that people are being cut off, the basic things they need as a human being.

I'll never forget the story that I heard about some gypsies that were invited to a convention. This was the first time that they had been invited to go anywhere outside of their little village. Check this out they get to their hotel, and they are checked into their room. This is the first time that they are in a hotel. They are blown away by everything that they see…the one thing that tripped them out was the fact that beyond the bedroom, there is a room called a bathroom. In the bathroom, there is a sink and a faucet. Blown away by water coming from this thing. The ladies said forget this convention we've discovered our purpose for being here. They unscrewed the faucet and knobs. Took it home to their village, put it on a rock, called everybody out there and said check this out. When they turned the knobs, and guess what no water came out. Why? Because when cut the source, you eliminate the resource.

I'll park here parenthetically because you got a whole lot of folk who are living in this country without any resources because they've been cut off from the source. Do you know what's like to live life without any sources to produce resources? It's one thing to sing Richard Smallwood you are the source of my strength, but it's another thing to wake up in the morning with no job, no light, no car, no money, and no hope. It's referred to as the High Cost of being poor. Although you don't pay with cash, you pay with stress. You can feel like you are peanut in a stadium being trampled over and over.

Our society has created a false narrative making it harder for undocumented civilians to live saying that they are criminals, and rapists, who need to be kicked out of the country. Innocent human beings are sitting in detention centers like animals in a shelter. Meanwhile as they changed the rules about DACA, the deferred action for childhood arrivals, saying that Congress has 6 months to fix it, or it will end. They changed the rules, and they keep telling you that its Mexicans who benefited from that program, it's anyone who is an immigrant who fled from their country for brighter tomorrows.

UNDERSTANDING THE TIMES

The NFL Blackout of which I'm so proud of my brothers and sisters. From Pastor Deblaire Snell in Huntsville, AL to others that are encouraging all Americans to not support the NFL with their dollar.

Now I'm not Blacking Out, because I want Kaep to get a job. I don't care how many rapists, abusers, liars, and cheaters are in the NFL, I don't want to put Kaep back in a system that said they don't want him, because at the end of the day more black boys will die, our girls will fade away without investigation, our schools will still be broken, and our communities depleted. Some cops will still act like they are above the law.

Those owners will still support Trump, those owners will still care about their special interest and their own own politicians. I'll boycott Robert Kraft and Tom Brady for giving Donald Trump an honorary super bowl ring, but will not denounce his illegal practices. I'll boycott Jerry Jones for saying, "I will never have a player on my team who will boycott the anthem." I'll black out John Mara and Steve Tisch who had nothing to say about Eric Garner when he was choked to death. Where was the Cleveland Browns owner when Tamir Ryce was murdered? Where was the Minnesota owner when Alton Sterling died? Where was the

Texans owner when Sandra Bland died and Abbot signed SB4? Where is the St. Louis owners when Officer Jason Stockley said he was going to kill Anthony Lamar Smith, chased him down and shot him at point-blank range even though Smith was not holding a weapon. I get it you like our bodies, because they fill your stadiums, and fill your pockets, but when there is a murder we have no words to say. Malcolm X told us, why in the world you would fight to sit at a table with people that don't want you there in the first place. Make your own table, then send them the RSVP.

UNDERSTANDING THE TIMES

I'm just trying to make this thing as real as possible. The times we are living in are terrible, turbulent, and treacherous. Hurricane Harvey, Hurricane Irma, and the other one that is cooking right now. People who have just purchased homes and a storm came in. People who just bought toys for their children, and now they are washed away. People who just bought a car so they don't have to take the bus to work. People who have just seen their keepsakes and memories washed away in a moment. People who did not have flood insurance...because you are aware of Texas House Bill 1774, which the Republican-majority Texas legislature passed during its most recent legislative session. The bill's supporters said it was meant to protect insurance companies from frivolous lawsuits after natural disasters. Detractors say it gives Texas property owners little recourse to get their money back if insurance companies don't pay up. Can you imagine that, natural disasters come in, FEMA funding has been cut, and now if you have a claim you have to fight in court, just to get not even enough to rebuild what has been broken.

UNDERSTANDING THE TIMES

North Korea is on a rampage testing out their nuclear weapons, that have the Japanese living in fear, but they are not the only nation acting out of the ordinary. The country of Burma the military are burning homes in ethnic cleansing. The Philippine war on drugs is a war on children, because of gun violence and mass shootings children as young as 12 years old are dying. Venezuela is still in a crisis, because of an unstable gov't, who has an unstable economy which has left its citizens without food, water, and adequate health care. Our brothers and sisters in Kenya must reopen their elections on Oct. 7 because of the opposition and rioting which resulted in unlawful killings and beatings by police.

The bible says that, for we know that the whole creation groaneth and travaileth in pain together until now.

The scripture compares the conditions of living in this world, to being like a woman in labor pain. Contractions of despair and worry, but I do know this that when you are in labor, the pain is prerequisite to a blessing. The pain is a process to the end that gives it meaning. You can't give birth to something new without some pain in your life.

Our scripture this morning comes to us from the book of 2 Chronicles, reminds of David's appointed men. In particular, it says that the Sons of Issachar had one job, and that is to understand the times and instruct Israel on what they ought to do. I love the text; the text says they understood the times. History tells us that these men were so intelligent that they were able to discern and comprehend the times that they were living in. They were David's trusted cabinet. They had discernment. What is discernment? I looked up the word, and I discovered that it means "to distinguish between, by sifting". One author puts it like this; Discernment is the ability to see things for what they really are and not for what you want them to be. I looked up the word, and I discovered that it means "to distinguish between, by sifting". If you know anything about sifting flour it's not an easy process; it's requires a lot of shaking, hitting, and passing through some small wires.

Discernment understands that the voice of God will never contradict the Word of God. Discernment can look at people and determine whether the people around you are there to feed the soil or just grab fruit.

Discernment will tell you never trust anyone who is friends with your enemies.

Discernment will tell you that I don't need a lot of people around me, because sometimes the people that are with you, might be against you…because at the end of the day I'd rather have 4 quarters, than 100 pennies.

I wish we had more men and women who are praying for discernment, and knew what to say, and when to say it. I wish some of them would just stop talking, and start listening to Jesus; then He'll give you something to say. Nobody wanna hear about half the stuff the most of us talk folk. What has happened to us, we don't even know when to shout, stand, or praise. We shout on trash and get quiet on truth. We will applaud ignorance, and get appalled by substance. We will praise someone putting on a show while they singing, and fall asleep when the gospel is being preached. We have no understanding or discernment of the times. Our theology has been hijacked by gospel pimping preachers of prosperity. We have subjugated God to a jeanie in the bottle that we just rub when want a blessing. We have surrendered church to solicit emotional fanfare, instead of intellectual stimulation. We care more about evoking feelings, and how high you jump instead of how straight you walk. We have stopped giving our members things to think about we just leave them feeling good. Our meetings are always revolving around more tithe, rather than more time saving and restoring humanity.

The bible says in the original language it reflects the presence of intelligence and wisdom, even cunning and skill, in the process. In other words, this is not just an understanding of the facts, but a skillful analysis of what something truly means.

Check this out; this is for you. Little to nothing is known about sons of Issachar, but Isaachar their father is one of the sons of the many sons of Leah. If you remember Leah was Jacob's wife. She was the wife that Jacob did not love, but she kept on having sons for him. She was giving Jacob loving while she was hurting, and every time she had a baby for Jacob, she would give them a name hoping that Jacob would love her more. Till finally she got smart and after the third baby she said, forget that if that negro don't wanna love me, I'm gonna love me, because I know that God loves me. That's when she had Judah, and she named him that, because she said, "This Time I will Praise the Lord. Then she had Isaachar, and Isaachar's name means "There is a Reward". The sons of Issachar are cognizant of their history, and their name. They know that their Mother was hated and rejected, but in spite of her rejection, God blessed her with a reward named Issachar. Therefore, the sons of Issachar are living up to their name.

I wish there was someone in here, who would recognize although you had a rough past, you got a better future, because of the long-lasting legacy that you come from. You got a legacy that will inform your identity. Once I know who's and who I am, there is nothing that you can say that can stop me from living up to what God has called me to be. We've faced rejection, but God has rewarded us. We have faced pain, but God has given us power. We have faced heartache, but God has given us hope.

Weeping may endure for a night but joy cometh in the morning.

Yeah though I walk through the valley of the shadow of death, I will fear no evil.

I can do all things through Christ who strengthens me.

When the enemy comes in like a flood the Lord will lift up a standard against him.

Be joyful in hope, patient in affliction, and faithful in prayer.

Not only that sons of Issachar not only understood the times, but they knew what to do. They knew what to do because they were "WOKE". Ah, what do you mean by that? Stay woke is the urban linguistics for Staying Awake. To be Woke denotes a different connotation….

According to Dictionary.com, "woke" is the past tense of "wake" — as in, someone who is past the process of waking up. They're done with it. They've moved on. They've evolved from, you know, being asleep and hitting the snooze button 15 times. And frankly, that's a pretty accurate description of how "woke" is currently being used as an adjective.

The word informs us that you can't know what's going on, or what to do if you are sleeping. If you keep hitting the snooze button because if you keep sleeping life is gonna pass you by. But to stay woke is to stay in a mode of consciousness and perception. Because you can be awake, but not woke. Yeah, you could be moving, thinking, seeing, breathing, but you ain't woke. Ain't nothing worse than a clueless, uninformed people? My prayer every day is to deliver me from clueless people. Deliver me from uninformed people. Deliver me from people who ain't woke.

But you know what you can't be mad at some people, they are awake, but they ain't woke. You got people who are smart, but they act stupid. Kind of reminds me of this so-called 'smart guy' who was revered by so many but especially by Adventists. This guy I ain't gonna say his name, but he's known for his medical advancements, but instead of becoming the surgeon general, his black face is in charge of housing and development. He was a really smart guy, now he has become a Trumpet, and he is blowing words out of his mouth. The brother had the audacity to say that Poverty is a state of mind. And he's right, it is a state of mind, because that's a poor way to think about poor people. You got a poor state of mind if you think that people want to be poor, and they need to pull themselves up by their own bootstraps. Poverty is result of the thinking of the Have Gots. Poverty is system. Poverty is a product of American Capitalism.

The text says that they knew what to do. That word means 'manufacture'. They knew what to create. They knew what to make. They knew how to take what was given to them, put something together. They knew how to take all the things that they had sifted out through discernment and make moves. It's not what happens to you, but how you respond to what happens to you. Is what you do with what life throws you. I learned that if life throws you stones, you better catch them things and use them as your stepping stones. The text says they knew what to create.

I wish we had more woke folk in our church's that take the raw material of what life has given to them and create something new. I guess I gotta go there, what did Sean Carter say, don't die over the neighborhood that your mama renting, take your money and buy the neighborhood. Sean is basically saying, even though life has been rough on me, I'm going to play the hand that was dealt with me and flips the deck.

Stay woke...

It's time for us to wake up and stay woke. Know what to create. Time to build generational wealth, and legacy for our children. When will we understand that it's time to stop marching, and start investing. Create a society within a society. When we will open our own credit unions instead of investing in Bank of America which takes our money lends it to everyone else but us.

Stay woke...

It's about time we stop fighting each other and start recognizing the imago Dei that is stamped on all of God's creations regardless of whatever walk of life.

Stay woke...

I know that we are a people that is looking for imminent return of Jesus Christ, and we often talk about persecution, but recognize the persecution of your brothers and sisters through a false narrative and being thrown into detention centers will happen to you, if you can't stand for them, then why should anyone stand for us.

Stay woke...

Our world is turning colder and colder every day. There is wickedness in high places, and if we don't speak truth to power, and call out our senators and congressmen for being weak and scared, then we will see vigilante justice. That is more people will start taking matters into their own hands.

Stay woke…

For I saw another angel flying in the midst of heaven having the everlasting gospel to preach unto them that dwell on the earth saying with a voice like a trumpet, fear God and give glory to him for the hour of his justice has come….

Stay Woke…

And at that time Michael shall stand up. He that is filthy be filthy still, and he that is just, let him be just.

Sons of Issachar knew what to do. You probably saying I don't know. I need direction. Well when you don't know what to do, you serve a God that has already done for it you. You just learn how to lift your hands. Put a praise on it and…

STAY WOKE

Reflections

- What do you think it means to be awake and not woke?
- Understanding the times isn't easy to do without the Holy Spirit. What are some ways that you can ask the Holy Spirit to show the real issues in our world, versus what the media only wants to tell us?
- Leaving a legacy is so important. What are ways that you are leaving a legacy for those that are following in your footsteps?

PRAYER

Father, I acknowledge that these times we are living in aren't getting better. I pray that as the world turns that You will keep me in perfect peace. Please endow me with your Holy Spirit so that I can wisdom and discernment to understand the times.

AMEN

5

This Is My Story

Mark 5:18-20

And when he was come into the ship, he that had been possessed with the devil prayed him that he might be with him. Howbeit Jesus suffered him not, but saith unto him, Go home to thy friends, and tell them how great things the Lord hath done for thee, and hath had compassion on thee. And he departed, and began to publish in Decapolis how great things Jesus had done for him: and all men did marvel.

You really don't know what people are going through by just looking at them. You can be the life of the party, but on the inside, you are suffering saint. You could wake up on top of the world, and go to sleep with the world on top of you. Somebody said I feel like if I take one step forward only to take two steps back. One moment you are up, and the next you are down. Because if you, not careful life will push you to your limit.

Do I have a witness in here, that every now and then when it feels like you've got things going for you, that all of a sudden it can feel like everything is at odds with you. Can you leave you wondering is this thing working for me, or against me?

It's like the day that I went to the mall to return a shirt. There are people in front of me who are successfully making their transactions. Folks are purchasing their items and returning the items. As soon as I get to the front of the line, the young lady had a strange look on her face; I simply said I'd like to return this item. She responds by saying, sir, I'm sorry, but our system is down. I'm like what you do you mean it's down. Sir, I'm sorry we've been having internet issues all day, and the system has been shutting down, off and on. I'm sorry sir, but hopefully, the system will be back up soon.

Folks, please understand my predicament. I have to wait; my day is wasting away why because the system is not working. The system is not working for me, but check this out there are people who were in the same line with me, and they are shopping laughing and trying on clothes, why because the system has worked for them, but somehow the system did not work for me. But this is what makes matters worse, they could care less about me, or my situation, because the system worked for them. They were benefactors of a system that worked for them, so why should they care about me and the folks behind me the system granted them the privilege to move around freely.

I guess what I'm trying to say that in this yet to be united states of America there are those that are benefiting from the system, but then there are others who are left stuck like chuck by the system. That's what life is like for black and brown people in America. The system is down when you have blatant economic disparities. The system is down when you have schools in communities that are prison pipelines. The system is down when your lifespan is contingent upon your zip code. The system is down when you have a president who stood on a platform yesterday as he addressed police officers and encouraged them to be even more violent than they already are. Ain't insane how we can sit down and watch diplomacy, decency, and dignity go right out of the door. Instead, we have replaced it with xenophobic rhetoric, scheming, underhanded, back-stabbing, foul mouthed, bully pulpit politics. The system isn't working!

I'm gonna hang out here, because in our text this afternoon we read about a young man who was away from home, living in the mountains cutting and hurting himself, full of many demons. Living on the bottom...This young man was sent to live in the mountains because nobody wanted to deal with him anymore. His teachers would look at him and figured that he would amount to nothing, so they had a low tolerance for him. He would run up and down foaming at the mouth and slashing himself with stones. Since they did not know what to do with him, they decided to lock him up. Because they felt like they could not control him, they deemed him as nonfunctional in the world that we live in today.

The same thing occurs today. Society has an answer for reckless young people, instead of rehabilitating them the answer is to lock them up and throw them in prison, send them away so that we can forget about them. Instead of training and teaching them, the answer is we've got room for you, in a gated community, and we will also give you a job that pays either below the minimum wage, or you will get no wages at the end of the day.

The Bible describes this young man as someone spent his nights and days hurting himself why because he is going out of his mind.

When you are disconnected from God, you engage in behavior that is destructive. I don't care who you are, and how good you think you got things. The further you stray from God, the more detestable, and unthinkable things and thoughts you begin to have, but you don't see it while you are doing it. That's why you come into relationship with Christ, and you look back over your life, you begin to say if it wasn't for the mercy and goodness of God I don't know where I would've been. You begin to think about all the things that you used to do, and who you did it with, and that's why your soul cries out hallelujah. I'm sure that there are times when you have looked back over your life, and you had to ask yourself was that really me!

Further along in the text, the word tells us that as Jesus stepped on the mountain, the demon possessed man ran to Jesus and bowed down before Him, and begged Jesus, this is not our time to be tormented.

Can I stop here to simply remind you, what kind of power you are working with? The text says that the demon runs to Jesus bows down before him and asks not to be tortured. I don't know if you've ever read this story, but we just highlighted the fact that he was sent to the mountains because no one could control him. Now demons supernatural beings are bowing down and worshiping God. They are basically saying, we know who you are. We know what you about. We know what you do. We know that power belongs to you, and you could wipe us out right now, but according to the scriptures, it's not time for us to die.

Demon recognize the deity of Christ. There recognize the awesome rulership and power of the

God we serve, and just to get us to stand up during worship, or kneel during prayer is like pulling teeth.

I don't know about you, but you ain't gotta push me, prick me, or poke me to acknowledge a God that could turn water into wine.

A God who can part a red sea. A God who can put some lions on a fast. A God who can cool a fiery furnace. A God who woke me up this morning. Started me on my way, and still finds a way to make a way out of no way.

Then Jesus commands the spirit to come out, and asks Him what is yo name? Jesus commanded the demon to come out of him because my problem is not with the young man, but my problem is with you. I'm not gonna blame this young person for his behavior, but I'm gonna blame demonic influences and strongholds for the reason why he's acting like that, or she's dressing like that. Aren't you glad then when you were out of mind, Jesus still dealt with you, instead of judging you. As a matter of fact, he's the only person that is worthy to judge me.

Jesus asks the Demon what is your name? The demon responds by saying our name is Legion because we are many. It's not just one of us, but there are many of us.

Truth be told I probably don't know the real you, but there is a truth in that for many of us, that there is more than us inside of us.

Jesus asks, "What is your name?" The demons respond by saying that our name is Legion. Now Legion was not the young man's name, but it was his problem. The reason why some of us struggle the way we do is because when God asks us what is your name, we don't want to identify the problem we are dealing with.

You will never overcome your demon until you identify it for what it is. Name your demon... Is it drinking? Is it fornication? Is it pornography? Is it anger? It is cursing? Is it cheating or lying? Whatever it is...Name your demon...

By Mark using the term Legion, he is also describing Roman Occupational forces. You understand that

Rome was controlling Israel, so by this young mans story is his testimony of how all Israelites were feeling living under Roman oppression. They were colonized. The young man is calling himself something that he is not. Colonialism creates an atmosphere of living death which fosters a systemic breakdown of the human personality. People who are colonized are conquered. In reality, they ask the same question "who am I?" Since they don't know who they are, they identify with every name that the conqueror gives them.

Too much oppressive thinking is operating in his brain. Therefore, in order for him to be free, Jesus says I must deliver him from these oppressive thoughts.

We are not monkeys, the N-Word, B-word, the H word, lazy stupid or ugly. I will claim a name that God has given to me. Oh no, I will not subject myself to a history that only wants tell me about my slavery, and not my royalty. I will not be a second class citizen…I am somebody, because I am stamped with the image of God. Song of Solomon 1:5 that says I am dark but lovely. I am as beautiful as Zipporah; I am as strong as

Ebed Melech I am as generous as Simon of Cyrene that carried the cross of Jesus. Excellence is a part of who I am. I don't have to borrow it from somebody. There's excellence in my DNA. I'm like Kendrick Lamar; It's in My DNA!

>I transform like this, perform like this.

>Was Yeshua's new weapon

Jesus says, I gotta do something for this young man...

Well Jesus says, party is over, ya'll get to get up out of here.

When this young man out of his mind approaches Jesus, He heals him and removes the demons from his life. Jesus said this is going to take an inside job.

The bible says that the demons asked for Jesus not to kill him, but to send us into the pigs.

A lot of you are the way you are because you keep feeding those pigs.

My daughter has this book called if you give a pig a pancake. If you give a pig a pancake chances are he's gonna want syrup, and you will give him syrup. If you give a pig syrup, chances are he will want a fork....

I've realized that for some of us in relationships it's like this. If you give a pig, a touch chances are he's gonna want to hug. If you hug a pig chances are he's gonna want a kiss, if you kiss a pig, chances are he's gonna invite you to the pig pen. Don't give a pig a chance.

The word tells us that after Jesus called the demons to come out of the man, they went into the pigs, and the pigs ran into the water. But did you know this? According to Dr. Frederick Haynes, that this is a kosher community, and swine is hanging out here? Did you ever stop to realize that there are jews feeding pigs, and using them for their own personal gain.

By the Jews keeping and feeding these pigs, according to one minister it represented an underground economy because wherever there is poverty, there is some shady business going on. Pigs are being fed in our communities. Our job is to open our eyes, and identify the pigs in our communities, that aren't helping us but are hurting us, and our children.

Payday loan advance shops, pawn shops, cheap malt-liquor stores, processed food stores, mama's fried chicken. Everything that is created to exploit and destroy poor people are in their communities, and it's up to the church to not just simply engage in charitable events, but we've got to be committed to breaking down systems and structures that exist to keep the poor poor.

By Jesus getting rid of the pigs, not only was he cleaning the man, but he was also cleaning up the community…by cleaning up the community, he was messing with their money…that's why they wanted Jesus to leave because on pig cost a whole lot of money.

GOD FIXES YOU ON THE INSIDE, SO YOU CAN BE USED OUTSIDE

God will deal with the demons that are controlling you, and then he empowers you to be a witness to those who were trying to oppress you. Before he was identified by his struggle, now he has a new identity in Christ.

Verse 19…The demon-possessed man begs Jesus to go with him…and Jesus says no.

As the great preacher William D. Watley once said, God will never give you a NO without an Instead!"

I guess it's safe to say that God doesn't always allow you to do what you want to do. It's safe to say that God isn't always going to answer every one of your prayers. God is going to say no sometimes because He wants you to say YES to the plan He has for your life.

DON'T EVER PUT A PERIOD, WHERE GOD PUTS COMMAS

JUST BECAUSE GOD SAYS NO, DOESN'T MEAN THAT IT'S NOT OVER..

Every now and then God will close doors in front of you because He's opening a better door for you.

The Bible says, Go home to thy friends, and tell them how great things the Lord hath done for thee, and hath had compassion on thee.

Jesus basically told the man that I've got enough with me right now, and I'm working on these, but go back to the place that you were planted and grow. God back home. Go home and tell your story.

The bible says that he went back home to Decapolis and told his story. I had to break down that name Decapolis. Decapolis is made up of two words. Those two words are Deca and Polis. Deca means ten, and Polis means cities. So essentially he went to 10 cities and turned those places out, with his story.

His story was so powerful that it turned those 10 cities upside down and the name, and following of Jesus grew to outstanding and large numbers, and the most churches were in the capital. Just a bunch of people on fire for Jesus Christ. You ask!!!!!

The ten cities were Gerasa, Scythopolis, Hippos, Gadara, Pella, Philadelphia, Capitolias, Canatha, Raphana and the capital city Damascus.

Preacher what in the world did you just say! You said that the gospel had grown so much in Damascus that there was an explosion. Did you know that Mark used Paul as a source for some of his gospel? If my brain doesn't fail me right now, but the last time I checked my bible, there was a man by the name of Saul who was on his way to Damascus eager to kill, persecute, and arrest those Christians.

But on his way to the Damascus, he was struck down by a bright light, and Jesus knocked him off of his horse, blinded him, and said why are you persecuting me? Anyhow Acts 9 is known as Paul's conversion story. And all of this transpired because a once demon-possessed young man was healed by Jesus and went back home, and shared his story. He owned his story.

He shared his unfiltered story and gave as it is. Can I tell you today, that you ought to own your story? Don't ever hide or be embarrassed about your story? Own your story, as a matter of fact, you can't start growing until you start knowing that God gave you that story for a reason. I've discovered that one of the signs of Christian growth is when you can share your story.

Telling our stories is not an end in itself, but an attempt to release ourselves from them, to evolve and grow beyond them. We tell our stories to transform ourselves; to learn about our history and tell our experiences to transcend them; to use our stories to make a difference in our world; to broaden our perspective to see further than normal; to act beyond a story that may have imprisoned or enslaved us; to live more of our spiritual and earthly potential.

Embrace your story because that's who you are! At the end of the day deep down we are all the same.

Reflections

- The young man called himself Legion which wasn't his name. How important is it for us to call ourselves the names that God has given to us?

- Can you identify some of the pigs in your community and in your life, and what ways can you be mobilized to remove them?

- We are changed when we hear the stories of others. What ways can you use your story, to help in the liberation of others?

PRAYER

Lord, thank you for my story, and may I never be ashamed it. Father I'm asking you to provide me with opportunities to share my story so that it can be a tool to liberate others.

AMEN

6

Dancing with the Scars

Jeremiah 31:13

Then young women will dance and be glad, young men and old as well. I will turn their mourning into gladness; I will give them comfort and joy instead of sorrow.

As long as I have been alive, I've never seen or met anyone who would welcome pain. Very few of us would even entertain the idea of, pain, affliction, heartache, and sorrow. Not too many of us embrace pain or do we run to it. Just the mention of the word can send chills up our spine. I strongly doubt that anyone of you during intercessory prayer said Lord bring some affliction into my life.

But to be honest, in some way, shape, form, or fashion, it is safe to say that we have all dealt with some type of affliction in our lives. For some of us up in here today, 2017 can be categorized as an afflicting inducing year. Pain and sorrow has shown up at your doorstep more than once. Has showed up at your job. Has showed up in your car. Has showed up even at church. Sorrow, Pain, and Affliction is no respecter of person. Affliction, when it comes, can leave us broken, battered, bruised, and scarred.

2017 has been an afflicting, and pain producing year. You lost some things in 2017; you lost some people in 2017. You may have lost your job in 2017, and all these things have left you scarred. Sorrow, Pain, and Affliction can you leave you torn battered and scarred.

Can I tell you a little bit about Jeremiah. Jeremiah was the name that his mama gave him, but the streets called him "The Weeping Prophet". The author of the book of Lamentations, God gave him a word to preach unto the children of Israel. History tells us that God called Jeremiah when he was young a man, somewhere between the age of 18 and 21. In chapter 1 the Bible says that the word of the Lord came unto him saying, *Before I formed you in the belly I knew you, and before you came out of the womb I set you apart to be a prophet unto the nations."*

In other words, before your parent's parents were listening to Ron Isley, I saw you and gave you a purpose. May I stand here today and testify that there is not a person on this great earth does not have a purpose. I don't care who you are; I don't care how you were born, how many pounds, you weighed, what kind of parents you have, or didn't have YOU BELONG HERE! And it does not please God to know that you will choose to live beneath your potential. Ain't nothing worse than a person who lives down to people expectations. Who will subject themselves to every thought and breath of what people around them think about them. Or a person who always feels like they have to prove themselves whenever they are around other people. The only person's opinion that you should care about is God. Because at the end of the day all these people around me don't got a heaven or a hell to put me in.

As long as I know that God says, I am the apple of his eye. He has loved me with an everlasting love. Lo, He is with me always. As long as I know that he walks with me and he talks with me along lines narrow way, that's all I need in order to have a good rest at night.

Then Jeremiah says, uhhh God, you sure you got the right Jeremiah, I'm too young. Then God claps back, He says Don't say I'm too young, for you must go wherever I send you and say whatever I tell you. Don't be afraid of the people, for I will be with you and will protect you.

Stop looking at what you don't have, and start thanking God for what you do have. I've discovered that a lot of us don't grow because we don't know what we've got on our side. A whole lot of us don't realize that we got more fighting for us, than what's against us.

Jeremiah was born into a priestly family in the town of Anathot in the southern kingdom of Judah in a period of religion and political turbulence. He has to grow up while preaching in the midst of two ravenous world dominators Assyria and Babylon. Not only does he have oppression from the government, but He is called to preach a message of repentance to a people who were not trying to hear it. He was called by God to go to people and places where he would rather not have gone to proclaim a persistently offensive message. His own people won't even listen to him.

After a while when you keep reading the book of Jeremiah, he gets fed up. In chapter 20, Jeremiah pours out his frustration before the Lord.

He says,

You pushed me into this, God, and I let you do it.

You were too much for me.

And now I'm a public joke.

They all poke fun at me.

Every time I open my mouth

I'm shouting, "Murder!" or "Rape!"

And all I get for my God-warnings

are insults and contempt.

But if I say, "Forget it!

No more God-Messages from me!"

The words are fire in my belly,

a burning in my bones.

I'm worn out trying to hold it in.

I can't do it any longer!

Then I hear whispering behind my back:

"There goes old 'Danger-Everywhere.' Shut him up! Report him!"

Old friends watch, hoping I'll fall flat on my face:

"One misstep and we'll have him. We'll get rid of him for good!"

He says, God, you took advantage of me because you are stronger than me.

I didn't ask for this, but you placed this upon me, and by you giving this to me I am now a public joke.

What if the person that gave you your scars was God? Every time I open my mouth, and I try to do what's right they ridicule me and laugh at me because the messages and the prophecies you have given to me have not even come to pass. There is a "Whisper Campaign" carrying on behind my back.

God, I didn't ask you to be a pastor. God, I didn't ask you to be a leader of this department, as a matter of fact, a small group of people called a nominating committee called me after they said that they prayed about it and suggested that I should be the face of this department. When I said yes, you didn't tell me that I have to lead a bunch of stubborn people that are stuck in their old ways.

When I signed up to follow you by being baptized, and joining this church, I did not expect my marriage to fall apart. I did not expect my family to break away. I did ask for these many deaths to come my way. I did not call you, email you, text you, I did not rap on your door, or tap on your window pane, you called me!

I got these scars. I got these bruises. I got this pain. But in the midst of those verses I could not help but recognize verse 9, *Jeremiah said I will not make mention of Him, Nor speak anymore in His name." But His word was in my heart like a burning fire...Shut up in my bones, I was weary of holding it back, and I could not.*

In other words, I tried to give up, and I tried to walk away, but I could not, because his word was like fire inside of me churning and burning inside of me, and I could not keep my mouth closed. I could not sit down on it. I could not hide it. So, in spite of all that I'm going through I will still declare your goodness and your glory. Although Jeremiah is afflicted, a man of sorrows, pain, and scarred. He says I can't stop. It is almost as if this pain is pushing him, growing him, and strengthening him for the fight ahead.

Is there anybody in here today who can testify that your pain is not there to take you out, but it's there to bring you up. Your scars are not there to make you bitter, but it's there to make you better. Can you see the moments when you were afflicted by some burdensome catastrophe, some calamity, some heartache, drew you closer to God, and has driven you in the presence of God and brought you into the sanctuary lift up both hands and say the Lord will make a way somehow! You can learn some things when the rain is falling that you can't learn when the sun is shining. You can learn some things when you are in the valley, then when you are on the mountaintop. There are some things you learn when the money is funny, and the change is strange. It has taught you that God can, and God will do for you what you can't do for yourself. Sometimes God had to put some things in your life in 2017 to prepare you for 2018. That God had allowed to go through certain things because God was saying I got to sit you down, shut you up, straighten you out, and got you away from everybody else because He had to teach you that you can't walk into 2018, the way you started 2017.

Every now and then I would watch my mother in law cook in the kitchen. We noticed that she would use this old burnt up pot. So I said to Carlene she has some nice new pots, nice shiny silver pots. Brand new state of the art non-sticking pots. Why won't she use those pots, why does she keep going back to the old burnt up looking thing. Carlene then told me that there is value in that old burnt up looking pot. Those new pots have never been burned, never been used, never been proven. You can't cook anything in that...But you see that old pot its full of scratches and all the signs of wear and tear; it has all the evidence of having been in the fire and come through.

Is there anybody out there who can testify that I've been through some things. I've got some scars and some scratches, but I've learned through it all to give God praise through my pain. Because he's got me on this fire, but I gotta realize that he's molding me, he's training me, he's preparing me, he's shaping me, he's rearranging me, he's humbling me, he's teaching me, he's leading me, he's squeezing me, he's training me, he's developing me, so He can use me for His Glory!!!!!

Jeremiah says even with these scars; I'm still going to do what God has called me to do. Can I tell you a little bit about some scars. I was reading about Misty Copeland. If you don't know Misty, then let me tell you a little bit about her. Misty is one of the baddest ballet dancers out right now. Misty who overcame adversity and obstacles to get to where she is right now. Misty, she is an African-American women in a field that there aren't many of, but this thing about Misty, Misty's first trainer said that you wouldn't make it as a dancer because of your body. You too thick Misty. You got too much going on. But even though Misty had an early setback, she didn't let that stop her. She worked hard, trained hard, studied harder, and now she is where she is. She had been through a lot of pain from a tender age. But as I was reading the story of Misty, and she was preparing for a big dance as she was in front of some other aspiring dancers, one of the girls saw some bruises on her legs. They asked her what happened; she said that she got it, from falling down in practice. The dancer then asked Misty are you going to dance like that, Misty simply replied and said sometimes you gotta learn how to dance with the scar.

And that's my word to somebody up in here today. What is a scar? A scar is evidence of something that has happened to you in the past, but it's still with you. A scar is a reminder of something that you have been through and hurt you. All of us have some scars. It don't matter how long you've been going to church, how big your bible is all of has been through something that has happened to us. But your scars should never stop you from giving all to God.

Check out the text this morning. Lets go to this poetic passage. Obviously we have been dealing with the earlier chapters of Jeremiah, and now we are in chapter 31. It's evident that Jeremiah has not given up. God gives Jeremiah some hope. Scholars refer to chapters 30-33 as God's Great Homecoming Party. What is a homecoming, a homecoming is traditionally a party of people that have been scattered all over the world get together and share experiences. Traditionally homecoming usually happens before a big event, usually a football game. It is a precursor to the venue. It is a get together before the event.

Jeremiah 30, Behold, I will bring back the captivity of Jacob's tents…

Jeremiah 31:8 says, Behold, I will bring them from the north country, and gather them from the ends of the earth, the blind the lame, the pregnant, the orphan. Everybody is coming to God's Homecoming….

Now jump down to the scripture reading verse 13, it starts off by saying "Then". After everybody has been gathered together and they are sharing their stories about exile, pain, sorrow, and scars, they begin to remember that God said, For I know the thoughts that I think towards you, thoughts of peace, to give you a future, hope, and an expected end.

Whenever the word "then" is used, it is to point you to the next scene.

To point you to the next immediate event. What is the next event? It is a party! It is a celebration. And at this celebration there requires dancing, the virgin will rejoice in dance. C'mon now don't act like you've never been to party, everybody loves a good time

I'm not sure if you realize, but these folks have been brought out of slavery, they have been through something, they are going to dance with the scars. Now, I know for some of us we have a hard time with dancing, we have issues with clapping, standing, and raising our hands in church. We have issues with dancing, and that's because Greek Philosophers have influenced our Theology and said that God is above our ordinary praise and He does not like that. Now I know why they did that because they can't dance they can't hold a beat. They can't sing and clap at the same time; they have to concentrate and think about it. And often times when people can't do something they demonize it and trample upon it. But you can't take dance out of Africans, Blacks, South Americans, the Latinos, the Caribbean.

So, you could sit there all you want and look as holy as you wanna be, but you know you got a dance inside of you. I don't know about you, but every now and then when I hear a good song, like Thank you Lord for all you've done for me, When I hear a good song like Never would've made it, when I hear all my good days, outweigh my bad days, my feet begin to start tapping, my head starts rocking, my shoulders start moving, and then I just gotta get up and express myself. Whoops, there goes my seat...

I got a dance inside of me, because if I should die before Jesus returns, but while I'm sleeping in my grave, and I hear that trump of the Lord and the voice of the archangel, the first thing I will do is jump up and down as high as I can.

You better find a way to praise God, because when ordinary words can't suffice. When words can't express the joy and pleasure that you want to extend to your God, then a dance will do. As a matter of fact, God does not have to do a thing because when I think about Jesus what he's done for me, when I think about Jesus and how set me free. I can dance dance dance dance dance all night.

Because if you knew what 2017 was for me if you knew what I had been through you would dance too. So excuse me, Mr. Conservative, excuse me Mrs. Judgmental, but if you don't get out of my way you, you're about to get hit why my two step. I dance because I'm happy. I dance because he changed me. I dance because he set me free. My shout is because he kept me. My hands are lifted because he has brought me out.

Notice that the text says, that the young men and old will dance as well. This wasn't any ordinary celebration. The text is specific and explicit that the men will dance too. In antiquity, only the women would dance. That's why when David was dancing it was disturbed Michal, not simply because you are a man, and your clothes fell off. David said look here lady thank God my dance wasn't for you, and I will keep playing music, and if I want to, I will be more undignified than what you just saw.

"IN BALLROOM dancing, the job of the man is to lead. The job of the woman, if her partner knows what he's doing, is to follow his lead. His job is to watch the floor and see where all the other dancers are. All she does is line up with his movement. She puts her hand in his hand. She puts her arm on his shoulder, and he sets the pace. She yokes herself with him, and as he moves, she moves. She kind of "with him and as he moves, she moves. She kind of glides and doesn't worry. But he has got to keep his eyes open. He's got to watch the floor. He's got to make sure that he doesn't step on her feet. She just moves in line with him. Now, she does move, but because she's yoked, she glides. He works.

Jesus wants us to know that He's willing to do the work. He's willing to take the lead. He's willing to guide and direct. He's willing to take us where we need to go, but we have to be yoked to Him. We have to be connected with Him and learn how to dance with Him. In doing so, we'll discover that He's gentle. He won't hold on too tight or choke the air out of us"

God says I will turn your mourning into gladness, I will give them comfort and joy. The word turn in the Hebrew means to demolish, overturn, and destroy. It's like God is distribution medication for your misery. I'll trade you, give me what you Got, and I'll give you what I have.

He says I will give them joy. I like that Joy instead of Happiness. Happiness can be a fleeting feeling, a passing presence, or a momentary memory. There is a stark contrast between happiness and joy.

Happiness depends on circumstances. Happiness depends on possessions. Happiness depends on monetary value. Happiness depends on moments.

But Joy is deep down inside. Joy says even if I don't have everything that I want I still got what I need.

Joy depends on the fact that God still sits on His throne.

Joy depends on the fact that though the storms of life are raging, I'm still trusting in the one who is the captain of the ship.

Joy depends on the fact that even though we walk through the valley of the shadow of death, we won't have to fear any evil.

That's Joy will be there when happiness is gone. Even when tears are falling Joy will still be there.

- Life changing joy.
- Power in the blood joy.
- Love lifted me joy
- Grace saved me joy.

- Goodness leads me joy
- Lily of the valley joy
- Rose of Sharon joy.
- Shelter in the time of storm joy.
- Rock in a weary land joy
- Peace in the middle of the storm joy
- Wonderful counselor joy
- Bright and morning star joy
- Hope for all believers joy
- I've got that joy joy joy deep down in my heart, and no man can take it away.

I gotta get out of your face. Let me leave you with this last story. CNN recently featured a story about how a poor, black woman saved enough money to purchase herself a home in Silicon Valley. She loved her new home. She kept the inside clean, and the lawn mowed. In an effort to get unwanted people out the neighborhood, the neighborhood association got together with the local bank and established a law that allowed a home to be foreclosed if the owner did not pay their association dues. For some reason or another, the black lady did not pay her $200 dues. As a result, the bank foreclosed on her house and sold her house which was worth over $100,000 for $10,000 to two white lawyers. The new owners threw her stuff out the doors and windows into the yard. She became homeless and had no place to go. Though she was homeless, CNN showed the woman in church that Sunday praising God. She danced up a storm. She danced so much until her dancing disturbed the minds of nine brilliant lawyers. The lawyers took her case to court, and they got her property restored. Whatever the situation, when you can't do anything else, you praise the Lord. Heaven can decipher what you need and take it from there.

Because when you learn how to dance with your scars, you understand and discover that the supreme one that you are praising has scars too. The Bible says, *But he was wounded for our transgressions, he was bruised for our iniquities: the chastisement of our peace was upon him, and with his stripes we are healed.* You are better because he was scarred. You are saved because he was scarred. You are redeemed because he was scarred. You are called because he was scarred. You're in this house because he was scarred.

Is there anybody in here gonna help me preach this sermon? I may not like what I'm going through, but I'm gonna praise him with these scars. I'm going to dance with these scars. I know you may not like it, but I know it's working for me, a far more exceeding and eternal weight of glory, and while I'm in it, I lift up both my hands and says Thank You. I will say glory to God. Hallelujah! I will lift up my hands, because when I do, Lord you catch me, and I am secure in the ark of the safety!

Reflection

- Do you feel that some of your scars are self-inflicted, or were they God inflicted, and how do you handle them?
- What's the story that accompanies your scars? Do you allow these scars to define who you are?
- Jeremiah wanted to give up, but he understood the difference between a 'calling' and a 'job', what do you feel like God is calling you to do on behalf of others?

PRAYER

Father, I've been through a lot and these scars that I have left me thinking that I can't be used. Teach me to trust in You, and to remember that I can still dance with these scars.

AMEN

7

Crisis In The Village

John 19:25-27

Standing near the cross were Jesus' mother, and his mother's sister, Mary (the wife of Clopas), and Mary Magdalene. When Jesus saw his mother standing there beside the disciple he loved, he said to her, "Dear woman, here is your son." And he said to this disciple, "Here is your mother." And from then on this disciple took her into his home.

In his critically acclaimed book entitled Ministry in a Danger Zone, by Dr. Alvin C. Bernstine states that the words uttered by Jesus in our text, are the only words Jesus spoke exclusively to the church while he hung on the cross. We are reminded that this awful, yet hope-filled and salvific moment at the cross was a disaster zone, yet it is was a moment which also was used to remind us of our obligation to our family, our community and our village.

Isn't it safe to say that our communities are replete with "disaster zones"—substance abuse, unemployment, economic downturns and financial fallouts, prisons that are disproportionately overrun with people of color, ineffective systems of education and young people who look at us as if we have dropped the ball because all too often, we have. The sad reality that for so many of us we live in these disaster zones. According to Donald Trump, we are living in Hell.

Trump's black and Hispanic hell is a dirty, trashy, rat-infested neighborhood full of barefoot, unemployed dark-skinned people who are all high off crack and strapped with state-of-the-art automatic weapons. These are very dark places-—the darkest of the dark. Sunny days don't exist. Now, there may be fresh watermelon stand in Trump's hell, but there are no schools, no churches, no scholars, no grandmas, no block parties, no cookouts, no dessert, no family structure, no success, no love, no hope. Trump's black and Hispanic hell is a dirty, trashy, rat-infested neighborhood full of barefoot, unemployed dark-skinned people who are all high off crack and strapped with state-of-the-art automatic weapons. These are very dark places-—the darkest of the dark. Sunny days don't exist. Now, there may be fresh watermelon in Trump's hell, but there are no schools, no churches, no scholars, no grandmas, no block parties, no cookouts, no dessert, no family structure, no success, no love, no hope. We don't read books, do yoga or eat salads in Trump's black and Hispanic hell. Hard work is a myth. These people are lazy and incapable of being educated, innovative or inspiring. Their only talents are frying chicken, rolling burritos and making babies whose lives are financed by the taxes he doesn't pay.

Yes, it may be bad, but please allow me to say this, not all of us are selling drugs. Not all of us are shooting up our neighborhoods. Not all of us are burrito, and fried chicken eating welfare recipients. We got Martin Luther Kings that came from our neighborhoods. We got Serena and Venus Williams that come from our communities. We got Lebrons, Carmelo's, and Kevin Durant's that come from our neighborhoods. We got a Michelle Obama's that comes from our neighborhoods. Instead of talking about the hell in our neighborhood, how about you talk about those that create the hell. MLK said we can't get mad at those in the darkness, but we must hold those accountable for creating the darkness. We got a lot of dark makers in this world. We got a lot of dark creators in these soon to be United States of America. Both republicans and democrats have failed us.

Redlining, and redistricting. Strict voter id laws. Flooding inner city communities with assault rifles. The proliferation of pawn shops, cash advance shops, liquor stores, fast food restaurants. No fruit and vegetable stands. Lack of jobs, lack of adequate recreational facilities. Loose dogs running rampant. Our communities are ignored community, blacks and browns are an ignored people. Our suffering is invisible. In order for it to be realized, somebody has to call us the N word, or someone has to shoot down an innocent 12 year old in a park, or someone has to massacre nine black people in a church, shoot an unarmed man as he runs from the police, leave a young man roasting on the pavement, kill a man in front of his girlfriend and a child for someone to shine a spotlight on what is happening. And when that spotlight is on upon, as they always have to catch us when we are at our worst. When our emotions are running high. Other than that the nation is unconcerned with the problems of America, ignoring the dimming eyes of black children waiting to be warehoused in the nation's prisons.

This darkness and disaster zone has taken a toll on our families. The black family in the church and outside of the church is struggling and striving to survive. Just trying to make ends meet. The family unit as we know it is becoming an endangered species. Divorce is on the rise, and yet we fail to realize that not only are there circumstances within the family structure that cause problems, but a whole lot of what is destroying the fabric of the family are circumstances that are outside that get inside, and will mess things up. It ain't just because of your family structure that you grew up with that is sabotaging our families, there's a whole lot attacking us.

One out of four African Americans live in poverty today. One out of three black children grow up in poverty, while only one out of ten white children lives in poverty. One of out of five black children are growing up in extreme poverty. That means that a child's parents can make less than 12,000 a year for a family of four which is 979 a month, 226 a week and or what ends up being 32 dollars a day. How appalling this is for a nation that considers itself the leader of the free world and pioneer of democratic principles, but you are contradiction? On one hand, you got nerve to vilify and demonize Colin Kapernaek for sitting down during the national anthem. The question must be asked, what is your national anthem to Trayvon Martin? What is your national anthem to Eric Garner? What is your national anthem to Sandra Bland? What is your national anthem to Michael Brown? Sit down Colin I'm with you because a few months ago we were celebrating that great athlete Muhammad Ali who basically did the same thing as Colin Kapernaek. You have declared a war on us, and we didn't even know that we were your enemy. Somebody has to sound the alarm…..

> I gotta go Benjamin Mays!
> I've only just a minute,
> Only sixty seconds in it.
> Forced upon me, can't refuse it,
> Didn't seek it, didn't choose it,
> But it's up to me to use it.
> I must suffer if I lose it,
> Give an account if I abuse it,
> Just a tiny little minute,
> But eternity is in it.

* * *

In all of this, the black and brown family has been dismantled and destroyed, by perpetual dysfunction. Historically slaveholders knew that the only way to destroy African Americans is to destroy the family, and the way you destroy the family is by cutting off the head. Eliminate the man. At times the master would rape the wife in front of her husband and children leaving the man defenseless. Or the master would kidnap the man, castrate him, then hang him in front of his family. Leaving the woman to manage and take care of her children. This would create the callousness in the woman because you didn't protect me from the master, nor did you fight back when he ran up in our homes.

Today it's the same thing, wives; mothers must watch as their boys and men have their manhood questioned and dehumanized in front of them. They must watch as they struggle from day to day filling out application after application to only be rejected by job after job. They must watch as government sponsored terrorism through police brutality, murder, massacre, or imprison them.

Our text this afternoon leads us to what I'm talking about. Jesus our Lord, Leader, and Liberator. Jesus, Heaven's Hero, Earth's Emancipator. Jesus lily of the valley bright and morning star rose of Sharon. Jesus, the way out of no way, is in a predicament at the moment. The text informs us that he is about to be crucified. As a matter of fact, the text says that he is near the cross. He is near the very instrument that has been created to destroy him. How in the world did he end up near the cross?

Jesus was a victim of an unjust justice system. A justice system that was set up for him to lose. A justice system that makes up rules as it met. An unjust justice system, one that says okay since you not one of us, you don't look like us, you don't have money like us, you deserve to be free like us. We gonna dehumanize you, and embarrass you in front everybody. Jesus is a victim of a criminal police system that set him up. That came armed and ready for war, they beat him up before his illegal trial. Hired liars, with a jury and judge that had made up their minds before the trial was over.

Such is the case with Jesus is the case today. We have a police system that has its origins in slavery. The institution of slavery and the control of minorities, however, were two of the more formidable historic features of American society shaping early policing. Slave patrols and Night Watches, which later became modern police departments, were both designed to control the behaviors of minorities. Members of the KKK infiltrated and joined the police after Jim Crow terrorism was made illegal. So black and brown have always been the target, and suspect. Terrence Crutcher walking back to his car with his hands up, only to hear the officer say he looks like a bad dude, we gotta put that thing down. Eric Garner, said I'm tired of y'all harassing me every day. Philando Castile, Freddie Gray, Oscar Grant, Michael Brown, Vinson Lee Ramos, Pedro Villanueva, Anthony Nunez, and even Jesus is a victim.

All of those names represent a member of a family who a mother and father must live without. The Bible informs us that Jesus' mother as she has to stand there and watch her son be given an unfair death penalty, and he is suffering before her very eyes...the word tells us that Jesus surveyed the crowd...He looks around and sees His mom....and in that moment Jesus puts aside his pain to speak to his mother.

Looking at our text within that context, one of the phrases which stands out is "standing near." The phrase stands out because

It occurs near the beginning of our Scripture, setting the tone and position of the participants and

This phrase of locality references the actual participants, those who are witnessing the awful culmination of wickedness and depravity being carried out by the Roman Government, which has partnered with the hypocrisy and machinations of the religious establishment, resulting in the exercise of capital punishment. The victim: Jesus.

Did you just read what read, machinations created by the religious establishment. Have you ever realized that some of the meanest people and most wickedest liars are folks in the church? I ain't got no problem with people outside of the church, I don't bother them, and they don't bother me. But church folk my God.

To dwell above with saints we love, that would be glory for me but to dwell down below with saints we know, that's another story….

The church set Jesus up, and let Rome execute him. It was the church that brought him to trial, in a business meeting, and said I so move that we have Rome Execute Jesus, is there 2nd to that motion. All in favor please say, "Crucify Him"

The church destroyed his family.

Please allow me to say this, Let me tell you something the crucifixion wasn't some private event, no this was on the busiest day in Jerusalem, so this was like putting it on the 6:00 news on every channel. You will be the international boogie man because we want to make an example out of you. We want you to know that it is illegal for you to go against the grain Jesus. It is illegal for you to spend time with the poor, empowering them, and humanizing them.

There is a crowd that has gathered, and in that crowd are some that are with him, and there are some that are against him. Can I hang out here homiletically, you gotta realize that not everybody who is standing around you is actually with you.

Lot of people will stand near you, beside you, and around you, but that don't mean they are necessarily supporting you, or riding with you

No folks will get near you, because it's easier to stab you, when I'm beside you. That's why you gotta check the folks that are around you. Not everybody loves you; not everybody is flattered by your looks, everybody doesn't think that you are funny, no there are some people that hate your guts. That's why Big Sean said, if they weren't with you during rehearsal then they need to be with you at the show. In other words, if you weren't with me when I was depressed, if you weren't there when I was struggling if you weren't there when I was trying to make ends meet then don't come around me when things are going good.

There were more who were against Jesus and wanted to see him die. They are those that believed the media account of his life. They are those that believed the concocted narrative that has followed his entire ministry.

But, the text says, "Standing near the cross were Jesus' mother, and his mother's sister, Mary (the wife of Clopas), and Mary Magdalene." Ahh, you gotta love those women...While the other disciples are scared and hiding, the woman go and stand, not only stand, they stand near the cross. There is nothing you can do to stop a mother's love for her son, that these women are willing to stand near the cross.

The original language defines this word stand as histemi. Histemi brings with it not just the understanding of "supporting oneself on the feet in an erect position," as defined by Merriam-Webster, but it also conveys a posture of maintenance, being firm, fixed and established. Histemi gives us the understanding of steadfastness coupled with an immovable and unwavering posture, in this case even in the midst of evil. With this in mind, the participants in our Scripture who stand near the cross of Jesus are remaining firm, focused, and unwavering. They maintain their posture despite the horrific scene before them.

They have the strength to stand in the midst of opposition. They are managing to stand in the midst of the pain.

I remember reading a story about a brother and sister who were playing with bozo the clown. They had tried everything that they could do to knock the clown on the ground, but it kept getting back up. Eventually, they got tired of doing all that they could. The sister asked the brother why in the world won't it stay down. The brother said, that's because there is something inside of the clown that you can't get too.

I don't know about you, but have you ever wondered how in the world you are able to stand through the most hellish situations. It's because you got something deep down inside of you, that the devil can't get too. It's inside of you. It's called the will to be all that God has made you to be.

It's called Greater is he that is in me than he that is in the world.

It's called no weapon formed against me shall prosper.

It's called for I reckon that the troubles of this present time are not worthy to be compared to the glory that shall be revealed in all of us!!!!

The word tells us that Jesus surveyed the crowd, He looks around and sees His mother, and in that moment Jesus halts his crucifixion, puts aside his pain to speak to his mother. He says, "Woman Behold Your Son".

Why did Jesus do that because Jesus knows that life for a single woman was hard in Jerusalem. Life for a woman that was a widow, and her only son is gone there is no bread winner. Jesus said you are my mama, you nursed me, you took care of me, you showed me, love, you gave birth to me and I ain't about to throw you underneath the bus…

How often do we as a people throw our sisters underneath the bus. Check that we throw them underneath the church bus….

All too often whenever it's time for dis-fellowshipping the young lady is the one getting the flames.

Every time we tell a woman that she is not good enough to hold a certain position you throw her under the van…

Every time you put a muzzle on a sisters mouth and tell her she is not worthy to speak you throw her under the church van…

Every time you misuse, and mistreat a sister in the church you throw her underneath the church van

How often do we throw our mothers underneath the bus…big old grown men living at home and you don't sweep no leaves; you don't cook no meals, you don't buy no groceries, you don't clean the bathroom. You disrespect the woman that gave you life. You got some sisters running around the place opening they legs to every tom, dick, and harry having babies, then make grandma take care of your kids while you in the club…

So, what does Jesus do…He, therefore, uses his hook up to hook up the unhooked…He realizes that a few hours ago I was your son…but right now I am your

Savior and Father...and since you look like you are down let me be your Lifter....

On his mother side he was born into this world, but on his daddy side he created the sun moon stars

On his mother side he would depend on her for water, but on his father's side he is the living water

On his mother side he would depend on her for bread, but on his father side he rained manna down from heaven

On your side, I would ask you to open doors for me, but on my father side, I am the door that leads to everlasting life.

On his mother side use would put him down to sleep and wake him up, bit on his father side he said I will lay down my life for my friends and in three days I will raise it up myself.

Jesus acknowledges his mother because history tells us that no husband and no son, was bad news for a woman in Jerusalem. She would have no defender. All land would be seized. Her rights would be stripped from her. For Jesus not to leave the example would contradict his word...

Isaiah 1:17, *Learn to do good; seek justice, correct oppression; bring justice to the fatherless, plead the widow's cause.*

Zechariah 7:9-19, *Thus says the Lord of hosts, Render true judgments, show kindness and mercy to one another, do not oppress the widow, the fatherless, the sojourner, or the poor, and let none of you devise evil against another in your heart."*

This is social prophetic gospel at its best...This is realizing a need and speaking to it...This is the gospel that Jesus calls us to do...This is putting aside ourselves for the sake of others...this is realizing that it's not about me, but it's all about them. This is soup kitchen hook up...

> This is a pantry hook up
>
> This is a homeless shelter hook up
>
> This is a mortgage refinance hook up
>
> This is resume writing hook up
>
> This is job search hook up

This is re-education for miseducation hook up

This is using your hook up to hook up the unhooked….

You also gotta remember that John is the only the gospel that records this word. Also, John is the only gospel that mentions the Miracle at Cana. Jesus said to his mother, "My Time Has Not Come Yet". Well Mother my time has come, and just like how I took care of you at the Wedding. I will take care of you today. I just want you to know in here this evening, the Lord is never too far to grant the requests you speak, and the requests of your heart.

I wish I had two or three people who could testify that if God had not hooked you up, you wouldn't be here today. Is there anybody in here tonight that's not afraid to testify that if it had not been for the Lord who was on my side, I don't know where I would've been. Is there anybody in here tonight that can say I was sinking deep from a peaceful shore, sinking to rise no more, but the master of the sea heard my despairing cry, and from the waters, He lifted me now safe am I.

Essentially when Jesus did this, He gave them something to hold them down until the day I return. He gave them something to keep them when the days hard and heavy, and the nights are dark and cold. Jesus was saying without saying keep this so that it can keep you. Take care of each other as I take care of you...

Look at the text. Although western culture views family in terms of DNA and biological constraints, in our African-centered context we know that family extends beyond the biological. For us, the family is our community, our village. With this in mind, the question is what will we, as a people, do to save our "Family" in the face of continued oppression, economic disparity, political machinations, and the continued slaughtering of our young sons and daughters? As Jesus hung on the cross dying, he gave instructions. "Woman," he says to his mother, Mary, "Here is your son." He then says to the disciple John, "Here is your mother." There were no adoption papers to be filled out, no guardianship to be recorded with the city clerk. Only the understanding that in order for the family, the village, the community to maintain its fabric of strength and resilience in the face of wickedness, there must be an acknowledgment of each thread, each person, that I am because we are, and we are because I am. It is the Ubuntu...I am only as good as you are, I am better because you are better.

The Bible says that Mary, mother of Jesus, along with his extended family, showed up and stood by the cross. Our question today is where will you be when the dirt goes down? Will you run like the rest of the disciples did in Mark 14:50? Or will you show up? Can you stand to stand at the crossroads when everyone has fled the scene? Can you stand at the crossroads when our sons and daughters have been mandated to carry and hang upon the crosses of this country? Will you say you'll be there because it makes for a good sound bite? The cross is not glamorous. You can't wear pumps or penny loafers at the cross; because the cross is not about keeping up appearances! Tailored jackets and ties are inappropriate at the cross. Battle fatigues are required attire at the cross. Squeamishness won't work at the cross. There's blood at the cross! And yes, there is destruction at the cross; but because the right ones show up, there's hope at the cross! There were far more who did not show up at the cross of Jesus than did. But those who showed up made a difference!

The Bible says that they first showed up! And when they showed up, Jesus acknowledged them, and then he spoke: "Woman, here is your son." In other words, I know you're here for me, but I need you to focus on who is next to you. I need for you to focus on your brother and your sister; I need you to focus on the extended family—the village. After she looks up, Jesus then instructs her to take her eyes off of him and look at John, who has no biological relation to either of them! So now she's got to look back down and see her new responsibility. Her starting point is to show up and stand. Then she has to look to Jesus, the author, and finisher of not just her faith but her community's faith as well.

Brothers and sisters, when we look up to Jesus, he will give us our marching orders. When we look up to the cross, we will understand our assignment. At the cross, Jesus is rearranging our family tree. At the cross, we behold the beloved community. At the foot of the cross, Jesus is calling us together. In my sanctified imagination I can hear Jesus saying, "Walk together children, don't you get weary. Work together children, don't you get weary, there's a great camp meeting in the Promised Land!" But the good news is that this promised land is not in the sky, by and by. When we show up, and look after each other, with our eyes on our Savior, the promised land is now; it's within us!

If Jesus is so concerned about his family, then what makes you think he doesn't care about yours, but you got to come near to the cross.

Family in crisis. Come near the cross

Are you hurting? Stand near the cross.

Reflection

- When there is a crisis in your village how do you respond?
- Often times a lot of our issues that we face stem from the kind of families we were raised in. When you think about your family, were they a stumbling block that hurt you or a stepping stone that helped you be who you are?
- When you think about the work of social justice as a biblical mandate in what places do you believe that God is calling you to stand?

PRAYER

Lord, there are communities that have been tarnished by policies and laws that take advantage of the weak. Please use me in whatever capacity to alleviate the crisis that remains in our village.

AMEN

8

How to Get Away with Murder?

Rev. 6:9-11
And when he had opened the fifth seal, I saw under the altar the souls of them that were slain for the word of God, and for the testimony, which they held: And they cried with a loud voice, saying, How long, O Lord, holy and true, dost thou not judge and avenge our blood on them that dwell on the earth? And white robes were given unto every one of them; and it was said unto them, that they should rest yet for a little season, until their fellow servants also and their brethren, that should be killed as they were, should be fulfilled.

In case you didn't know, but there is a bad sister out there by the name of Shonda Rhimes. Her poignant pen has been used to write and produce the Thursday evening dramas Greys Anatomy, Private Practice, Scandal, and the latest phenomenon to hit the airwaves, "How To Get Away With Murder", starring the talented, gifted and beautiful actress Viola Davis, and I don't care what anybody says that sister can act. Viola Davis plays the witty, and extremely intelligent professor slash lawyer Annalise Keating, who is a no nonsense lawyer that always has to win every case she takes. Created to cause suspense, the show takes you on a twisted, yet backwards journey to discover the killer of a young single white female college student. In an appearance that is worthy of an Emmy, Viola Davis sits in front of the mirror as she takes off her wig, eyelashes, and makeup and asks her husband, "Why Is your picture on a dead girls phone?" More clues are pointing to the husband of Viola Davis yet still as you watch the show you are left at the end of your couch waiting for the next turn in the nighttime thriller, you are only left to wonder How To Get Away With Murder.

Even though TV land is riveted, captured, and handcuffed by the series, the reality is that in our yet to be the United States of America, they have always had the answer to "How To Get Away With Murder".

Do me a favor; I'm going to ask you to hit the back button, on your mental browser and travel back with me to July 13, 2013. Can you remember how you felt on that day? If you're having trouble, then allow me if you will to use some descriptive language to help you recall. Bewildered, baffled, perplexed, confused, angry, vexed, sad, and disappointed were just a few of the emotions that flooded our souls on that day. The verdict came from 6 women on that jury. It was not the trial of George Zimmerman, but it became the Trial of Trayvon Martin. A dead young man who wasn't even alive to defend himself.

There was Michael Dunn vs. Jordan Davis. A man just feels entitled to tell a group of young men to turn down their music, and when they refuse, he feels justified in shooting nine rounds into their vehicle and lied about the fact that they had a gun. Although he was convicted of four counts, well he should've been convicted of first-degree murder as well. He walked out of his vehicle, said I hate this thug music and took his gun with him.

And now we find ourselves at the same place, watching the television as we get news that another young man dies before the age of 21. He will not go to college. He will not get married. As his hands were up, he was gunned down in broad daylight, while his corpse laid on the streets for over 3 hours. Meanwhile, days go by before the murders name is released, and yet he his home drinking lemonade. He has not been charged with murder.

Then there is Eric Garner who choked to death as he screams to top of his lungs that I can't breathe. The officers use an illegal tactic to take him down; chokeholds are illegal, then they proceeded to suffocate the man, for what, allegedly selling cigarettes.

Tamir Rice a 911 call goes out that there is a young man in the park with a gun, but the gun looks like a BB Gun, as soon as the officers roll up they ask him to put his hands up, and before he raises his hands they unload a plethora of bullets upon him. Oh yes, my friends these are just some of the murders that we hear about...

The acquittal of Mr. Zimmerman, the trial Michael Dunn, the death of Michael Brown, the non-indictment of Officer Wilson informed us that race does matter, and black boys lives are meaningless. K. West said what's the life expectancy of black guys the system is working that's why. J cole. What's the price of a black man's life checked the toe tag not one zero insight.

Gays get their right to get married, but 11 states deny the right to vote to more than 10% of their black populations because of felony convictions and gave the right to enforce the voter identification law and redistrict maps that would change the way we vote from now on.

I guess it was a bad year to be an African American, but then again when isn't bad to be African American. It's kind of like what Melissa Harris Perry describes in her book Sister Citizen...In the book, she says that people are invited into a crooked room, with a crooked chair, and crooked pictures, and then they are told to stand up straight. Picture it, if you can see a crooked room, with a crooked chair, crooked pictures, and then asked to stand up straight. That's the sad reality of so many blacks in this world today; you are asked to stand upright in a crooked world that always finds a way to miscarriage justice. I personally believe that the term miscarriage of justice is a gentle way of describing it.

A miscarriage says that you have done your best to carry the baby, and then suddenly unfortunate circumstances cause you to lose what you've been holding onto...but an abortion says you don't wanna carry it, you don't want it, so you get rid of it. And that's what I see time after time...abortions of justice. Danroy Henry, who was driving away from a scene was murdered by an officer "abortion of justice", Oscar Grant who was shot in the back of the head, and the officer said I made a mistake I thought my gun was the taser "abortion of justice", what about Iraq in America, Chicago, Chiraq thousands of young black men dying every day because of gun violence, and yet still no one talks about the thousands of black and brown little girls that are kidnapped and forced to be prostitutes.

Months ago, Michelle Alexander wrote a moving article entitled Why black men are the permanent under-caste. She says, one of the reasons that these deaths resonated so powerfully with millions of people of color, black and brown and me in particular, is that it was one of those rare situations in this so-called era of colorblindness when suddenly the curtain was pulled back. All the usual rationalizations for routinely treating young black men as problems and up to no good, were made visible. There was just a young teenager on the phone with a girl, carrying a bag of Skittles and an Iced tea, and he was viewed for no logical reason as scary, out of place, and on drugs, then there was a group of young men just listening to Rap Music which is always played loud, minding their own business, and then a young man walking down the street, whom the officer had to yell at and say get out of the road, then there was the father on a street corner who allegedly selling cigarettes—but yet these are people who need to be confronted, interrogated, yelled at and put in their place.

Our criminal injustice system for decades been infected with a mindset that views black boys and men in particular as a problem to be dealt with, managed and controlled. "When you have a society that takes at its founding the hatred and degradation of a people, that society will inscribe that degradation and hatred in its laws and policies. When you have juries of 6 white women, and juries of 6 whites and 3 blacks what do you expect. It is painful to say this: Trayvon Martin Jordan Davis and Michael Brown are not simply an abortion of American justice, but it is an abortion of American civil rights itself. This is not our system malfunctioning. It is our system working as intended. To expect our juries, our schools, our police to single-handedly correct this for us, is to look at the final play in the final minute of the final quarter and wonder why we couldn't come back from twenty-four down."

I can't stand to hear people say blacks need to pick themselves up, they got their freedom, do something with but Lyndon B. Johnson from this very state said, It's like running a race, and you give your opponent a heads start how do you expect them to catch up….It's only about 50 years ago that we've been given the right to vote. After the emancipation proclamation was signed, white lawmakers designed what is called Share-Cropping it was slavery by another name. Check this out if you were black and free, and you were walking down the street, and you could not prove that you were working, you were locked up and forced back into slavery. If you were walking down the street and you didn't get out of the way for a white person, you could be arrested and forced back into slavery.

That's why African American's need to form their own unions, their own banks, their own police, and their own schools. We talk about not shopping on Black Friday, how about we show up on Voting Tuesday, and mid-term elections. If we gonna line up for sneakers, then we should line up to vote for our district attorney, our councilman or woman, our school superintendent, senator, and congressman. We must vote, vote, vote, not to ask them how we can work, but to say this is how it's gonna work. Blacks and Hispanics need to obtain more positions of power. Jews have their own thing; nobody calls them racists or separatists. The Dollar needs to start turning over in our community. They say the dollar touches 7 hands before it leaves the community.

We need to stop letting people who have no interest in our communities or people set up shop in our neighborhoods.

A now there is undercover racism. I agree with Richard Sherman that Thug is the New N-word. That's right when you hear the media call young black men thugs; they are calling you a Nigger. Ain't it kind of messed up that there was a hockey game, and right before the puck was dropped, they began fighting, knocking each other's teeth out, but yet still nobody calls them thugs. Nobody refers to them as violent and uncontrollable individuals. They are just playing the sport.

If you're not careful, the newspapers will have you hating the people who are being oppressed and loving the people who are doing the oppressing. Yes, they will show you videos of looting, burning, and fighting, but they will not broadcast the peaceful demonstrations and folk in the church praying.

This is bad news for people of African ancestry, sending a global signal about the criminalization of African Americans, especially African American males.

It's kind of messed up because Black Men are always treated like a threat. Black men are always treated like we are about to do something violent. Don't you think it's terrible that we are the only race that has to advise our children how to act when they see the police. We are the only race that has to set up seminars and write books about how to love yourself and treat yourself. We the only race that gotta tell black boys you gotta be twice as good just to sit at the table. Ain't no other race spending this much money just to survive in America. Ain't no other race gotta worry about how they are portrayed in the media. We the only folk that realize that black men are an endangered species.

And that's where I wanna hang out today. Revelation 6:9-11, gives us a full pictorial view of injustice. As a matter of fact, the author of the book of Revelation John is a victim of injustice, by the justice system...A man who is trying to stand up straight in a crooked room, with a crooked chair, and crooked pictures of Caesar everywhere he looks. He was sent to the Island of Patmos simply because of word of God and his testimony. He was locked up on this island for no bad reason simply because He loved the Lord...He was locked up without due process. So, John writes from a prisoners perspective.

God shows him that there are times in order for me to get through to you, I got to put you on an island all by yourself.

The Book of Revelation was suited and designed "to give comfort and hope to oppressed and downtrodden" Christians in their frightening circumstances and to prepare them to meet further crisis.

In Chapter 6, he breaks the seals open...the first four are horses...white, red, black, and pale. But the fifth seal...is different.

John observes an altar...and under the altar are souls...and these souls begin to speak. The imagery drawn here is taken directly from the Old Testament sacrificial ritual and must be understood symbolically. As a matter of fact,, John borrows language from the book of Genesis...and if you remember in Genesis, there was some messed up things going on. In chapter 4:10 God says to Cain...What have you done? The voice of your brothers blood cries out to me....

It was always understood that when the blood of innocent people were shed, their blood cries out for justice. And that's real, the blood of so many innocent people that have been murdered physically, or mentally cries out today. The hands of our nation are stained with the blood of so many innocent people that they have willfully tried to silence. If you listen carefully can you hear those people who have died marching for their freedom? If you listen carefully can you hear those souls that have hung on the lynching tree?

So, the text tells me that you can't do WRONG to RIGHT people and expect to get away with it, especially to God's people. You will reap what you sow. Because life is like a boomerang, in my research I read that just as fast as you throw it, it will come right back to you the same way.

So, the blood of the martyrs are crying out, the Greek implies that they are shouting to God emphatically...they say How Long Oh Lord True and Holy? They say How long which suggests that they have been waiting for something to happen. They're getting tired; it's as if they are saying, God, we would appreciate it if you did something sooner than later.

The text suggests that Waiting Can be hard to do sometimes. Excuse me waiting on the Lord can be so hard sometimes. Especially when it seems like the unrighteous are always prospering. It's hard sometimes to keep reminding yourself that we are winners, whenever we keep losing so much. That we are victors when we are always victimized...We are comfortable, when we always feel conflicted.

How long O Lord, before you vindicate your name? How long will you allow the unrighteous to trample over your name?

O Lord true and holy? The martyrs are crying for justice, because they have been victims of injustice. It's like How Long O Lord True and Holy are you not going to act like yourself. To these martyrs it seems as if God is not acting like himself. It seems like God has become silent, dormant, and dead. Therefore, God must be busy, or simply not interested. Is your phone on vibrate, or do not disturb? Their expectations have not been met...who they have died for doesn't seem like He is doing what he said he would do. They are watching and waiting...they are watching and waiting….

They cry out O Lord How long before you avenge our blood? Avenge our blood. Church there is a major difference between revenge and avenge. Revenge is to get your own back for an injury you consider personal. Avenge is to get retribution for injury to another.

This may fit more with the theme of the sermon. To avenge is to punish a wrong with the idea of seeing justice done. Revenge is harsher and/or less concerned with justice than with retaliating by inflicting harm.

Her father avenged her death by working to have the man arrested, tried, and convicted, while her boyfriend took revenge by killing the man's wife.

The saints are such Christians that they are not even concerned with themselves, but they are crying out for others that will be hurt for the sake of being true to the gospel message. You know you are a Christian when you start praying for others. You know you are a Christian when you start praying for people that will experience the same thing that you have faced...And you say Lord have mercy on them and protect them from the pain that I have felt. Because you already know that what you got is greater than what anybody could do for you.

The text is telling me that they are asking God to avenge their blood...okay if you God is going to avenge their blood then He becomes an "Avenger".

Okay y'all tripping. There was a scene in the movie Avengers when Loki and Iron man were talking, and

Loki is going on and on...While Iron Man is calm and relaxed. Loki says we have an army, and Iron Man says we have a Hulk. In other words if you knew what I going for me, you wouldn't mess with me, cuz my God Is a bridge over troubled waters...My God is a way out of no way. My God holds the world in the palm of his hands. My God is able to keep me when the waters are trying to overflow me.

You got an army, well I got a Jehovah Jitendra

You got a navy, well I got a Jehovah's Nisse

You got an Air Force, well I got a God that neither slumbered nor sleep

You got marines, well I got a shepherd that will lead me through the waters, and they will not overwhelm me!

The text says he answers their plea. He opens his ears. And when he hears them, he answers their prayer in an unconventional way.

He gives them simultaneous servings....it's almost like God is the cook and the waiter. While he's cooking up a miracle, he's handing out mercy. While's he's preparing his goodness; he's giving out grace. I'm just saying that while God is preparing the ultimate blessing for all of us, in the meantime he gives you things to help you cope with what you are dealing with right now.

I liken this unto Tylenol Extra Strength 24-hour Pain Release medication. The medication is designed in a way that it releases relief in your body when you need it most. *Do I have a witness, that God has a way of releasing relief for our pain and misery when you need it most.*

He gives you the peace that passeth all understanding. He gives you life and life more abundantly. He gives pain relief that keeps reminding you to keep on pressing on.

But I've discovered that just because God isn't doing what we want him to do, doesn't mean that he's not doing anything at all.

The Bible says, "They are not crying for revenge, but they ask God How Long O Lord before you judge and avenge our blood?"

God's righteousness (or justice) is the natural expression of His holiness. If He is infinitely pure, then He must be opposed to all sin, and that opposition to sin must be demonstrated in His treatment of His creatures. When we read that God is righteous or just, we are being assured that His actions toward us are in perfect agreement with His holy nature

Justice, when used of God, is a name we give to the way God is, nothing more; and when God acts justly, He is not doing so to conform to an independent criterion, but simply acting like Himself in a given situation. . . God is His own self-existent principle of moral equity, and when He sentences evil men or rewards the righteous, He simply acts like Himself from within, uninfluenced by anything that is not Himself."

God says okay, let me give you something to hold you down...Hold you down is just language, that means this is going to keep you until I can give you, what is actually already prepared for you.

God decides to open His walk-in closet, beyond the priestly robes, Moses' rod, Elijah's chariot of fire, beyond the shield of faith, breastplate of righteousness, and the sword of faith...and on the hanger are white illustrious radiant robes are there for them.

Numerous studies have been done showing that when people are down, they would go shopping. There is something about coming home with something new... There's something about a new suit, a new dress, a new uniform; you just can't wait to wear it. You feel brand new...you look at yourself differently. But it's even better when somebody gives you an item for free. You appreciate it...you just love it.

Just stay in the fight long enough...God is going to come through...God is going to fight for you..

JUST HANG OUT AND WAIT

Rest for a little season, for a little while. I know right now things are not the way you would like them to be...but rest. I know right now that it feels like God has forgotten you...but rest. I know right it feels like you can face tomorrow...but rest.

Hold on my child, as a matter of fact, hold onto God. Trust God that you are willing to let Go of whatever is around you, trust God even when you can't trace him

Why, because this phrase in verse 11, until their fellow servants also and their brethren, that should be killed as they were, should be fulfilled. The actual fact is that these martyrs have died, and others will die as well for the sake of Jesus Christ. The text informs us that injustice will continue to prevail as long as it is in the hands of wicked men. More people have died and will die because someone with a crooked room, crooked chair, and crooked pictures will try to force you to stand up straight. Some of us in here today may die because of this word.

The sad reality is that many more African American men will die wrongfully. Men more men will be locked up innocently. Injustice will prevail, but I've discovered that after injustice after injustice it has to give birth to true justice at some time. Did you know that $-3 \times -2 = 6$ A negative plus a negative equals a positive.

Because when you keep having negatives, negatives negatives, it's gonna equal a positive. How is that the negative death of these young man has resulted in non-violent, positive marches around the world. How is it that the death of these young men has brought blacks, whites, Latinos and Asians together? A positive is coming out of this because at this moment people are fighting against the idea that you can have jury's with only a certain group having representation. A positive is that folk are lobbying Congress for stricter gun laws. These murders are starting movements.

These murders spark the movement. It doesn't mean that we should stop fighting…These murders should move us to social action, and social involvement. ….

In spite of injustice, we should still fight for the right…because that's what the bible tells us to do…*What does the LORD require of you, but to do justly, and to love mercy, and to walk humbly with your God?*

Although only 3 percent of churches volunteered in the civil rights movement, it was the mother of Emmit Till, who had an open casket funeral because she wanted people to see the injustice. It's time to Open up the casket for America. It's time to open up the casket of discrimination. It's time to open up the casket on inequality in regard to women's ordination. It's time to open the casket of injustice. It's time to open the casket on mass incarceration. It's time open up the casket wealth inequality. You can't get away with murder as Long God is sitting on his throne!

Reflection

- Was there ever a moment in your life when you felt like you were by yourself on island like Patmos? What do you think God is trying to communicate with you?
- Since the death of Trayvon Martin, there have been many more deaths. How have any of those murders moved you towards acts of justice?
- Trusting God is always a hard thing to do when you are in a difficult space. What ways are your learning to trust in God in the midst of injustice and pain?

PRAYER

Lord, as I see the injustice in this world, please use me in any way that You desire. You have called me to be Your servant. I know that you find no pleasure in murder, so please exercise your power through me to make a difference.

AMEN

9

Why We Can't Be Silent

Exodus 2:11-14
One day, after Moses had grown up, he went out to his people and saw their forced labor. He saw an Egyptian beating a Hebrew, one of his kinsfolk. He looked this way and that, and seeing no one he killed the Egyptian and hid him in the sand. When he went out the next day, he saw two Hebrews fighting; and he said to the one who was in the wrong, "Why do you strike your fellow Hebrew?" He answered, "Who made you a ruler and judge over us? Do you mean to kill me as you killed the Egyptian?" Then Moses was afraid and thought, "Surely the thing is known."

What a timely and startling message we find in today's world. Why we can't be silent? The title suggests to us that there is a call to be bold in the name of Jesus. The title perspicaciously puts us in our place if you will. Its magnanimity lies heavy within the minds of those that hear it. After all, the great poet and orator Robert Frost said,

> *The woods are lovely, dark and deep.*
> *But I have promises to keep,*

And miles to go before I sleep,
And miles to go before I sleep.

I have promises to keep and miles to go before I sleep, we have promises to keep and miles to go before we sleep. Because if we sleep, then the systems that have been set up to kill and destroy will prevail. We have promises to keep and miles to go before we sleep. Because if we sleep they will die. Who are they? The 'they's' are those that have been misused and abused by public policies that don't call you $\frac{1}{3}$ of a man, but will treat you like you are $\frac{1}{3}$ of a man. They are those that have been victims of not just Jim Crow apartheid, but Jim Crow had children and cousins. Janice Crow, Joey Crow, Jermaine Crow, yeah I said Jermaine Crow, cuz you got some of our own folk that will use all their power to hold you back than to open the door so that somebody else can walk inside. Who are they? They are those that find themselves in a new age chattel slavery, by the big business of prison cells, in a country that locks up more black and brown people than any other fully developed country. They are those that have been victim to gun violence not only in Chicago but across these yet to be United States of America. We have miles to go before we sleep.

That's why I celebrate, appreciate, and commemorate the memory, legacy, and life of Dr. Martin Luther King Jr. Mr. Luther King Jr was a drum major for justice; a silver tongued orator with a passion to see that others receive their right to life, liberty, and the pursuit of happiness. He was born on January 15, 1929, but on the next Monday of every month we salute his fervor and vigor. We salute the fact that as a young man he could not remain silent, as he witnessed the deprivation and degradation of his people he knew that a stand must be taken. Although crime was high, looting and rioting was everywhere. Martin Luther so eloquently said, "A riot is the language of the unheard."

Then in another instance as he was being interviewed by Mike Douglas, and as he was questioned about the crime in urban communities

Martin quoted from Victor Hugo, *"Where there is darkness crimes will be committed. The guilty one is not merely he who commits the crime but he who caused the darkness."*

We can't be silent when it comes to those that cause the darkness. We can't be silent when it comes to those that give money to gangs, in some cases also known as your local police departments to racially profile, and harass US Citizens every day. We can't be silent when we live in a world wherein you can measure the lifespan of someone simply based on their zip codes. We can't be silent when you have people that hold onto services that you need, but treat you like a credit card that has been maxed out. So every time you try to get access, you are denied. Access to college denied. Access to capital denied. Access to health care denied. Access to homes denied. We can't be silent; we must address the darkness that encapsulates this world that we live in. Not just in America but how about in India where it appears that it is legal to rape and victimize women until they die, and no one is brought to justice.

The word tells us that Moses had grown up. Pause, let me pull over park right here. The text tells us that Moses had grown up. Moses got mature, it's not until we decide to grow up, then we can begin to change things. When I grow up, I begin to show up, and show out. Currently, it's safe to say that we are grown when it comes to majoring in minors and minoring in things that are major. It's safe to say that we are majoring in programs and practices that don't benefit others than ourselves. When we do that we ignore the mandate that God has given to us in Micah 6:8 *"For he hath showed thee, O man, what is good, and what doth the Lord require of thee, but to do justly, and to love mercy, and to walk humbly with thy God? "*

God says, treat your neighbor the way you would want to be treated even if they are doing wrong to you because the God you serve will still bless you with favor that they can never give to you...

He says to love mercy, embrace it, date it, get to know it, as a matter of fact, you should know it already because if we're not for God's mercy you would have been dead right now. Mercy says you didn't get the punishment that you deserved for what you did, so how in the world you will not pardon those that have wronged you? How in the world will you not extend an arm of love to those that have said something dastardly to you? You love to be forgiven then why can't you do for somebody else. Then he says walk humbly with your God, in other words, don't take yourself seriously, take God seriously. Remember that you are the creation and He is the creator.

When the words of God's love are ignored, and the self-sacrificial life of Christ is trampled upon you forget the reason for our living and our being. You have the unmitigated audacity to pimp the life of Dr. Martin Luther King whenever the day comes every year. How in the world do we pimp the dream? The dream gets pimped when people choose to have big elaborate dinners honoring themselves instead feeding the least of these. We pimp the dream because it becomes heavy with commercialism and consumerism. We pimp the dream when we only remember once a year, but forget about it for the other 364 days in the year.

Moses had grown up, and as he was outside checking on his people, he saw the hard labor that they had to endure. He saw how Pharaoh's cold hand was upon his people, making bricks without straw. Exodus 1:12 says, the more they afflicted them, the more they multiplied. As he surveyed the land, he noticed the Egyptian beating down a Hebrew. Moses said, nah it ain't going down like that. Moses said you aren't just going to beat down on a defenseless Hebrew. You aren't just going to mess with my family; the word says that Moses looked left and right, when he saw nobody was looking he killed the Egyptian.

Now, I ain't telling you to murder anybody, but I'm not advocating or promoting the killing of any human being. We didn't create life in the first place, so we ain't got no right to take anyone's life, but if you will take the principle in this text, it is suggesting to us that whenever and wherever there is the injustice of people beating up, and beating down the defenseless we are rightfully called to step in take action. The Egyptian represented the methodical plot of slavery and abuse. So it's only right that the word for today is that you gotta kill the promotion and promulgation of mistreatment towards to the least of these. Racism is still alive and doing very well. It has morphed into different manifestations. It has morphed into ways that are subliminal and subtle.   Moses said I can't be silent. Moses said I just can't turn my head the other way and ignored this travesty. If he had turned the other way that would've been another dead person. Moses said I can't afford to let this brother die. I can't afford to let him fall by the wayside. I got to step in and lend a hand, even if it means that the hand that feeds me may get cut off. Even if it means that I may lose something that is so dear to me, it's gonna be worth it. That's why I appreciate and celebrate goodly, and Godly examples like Martin Luther King Jr, who did not think about themselves first, but found a way to help others.

Sacrifice, Moses sacrificed himself for the sake of somebody else who probably didn't know him. He sacrificed himself for somebody who he probably had no familial ties to, but just realized that he was a brother just like him. Moses sacrificed his good job, and Moses sacrificed his mansion on a hill. He sacrificed his status as an heir to throne, all the luxuries of life, women, and money.

As a matter of fact, he gave up what he had, to help someone who didn't have.   Hebrews 11:24 and 25 says, *By faith Moses, when he was come to years, refused to be called the son of Pharaoh's daughter; Choosing rather to suffer affliction with the people of God, than to enjoy the pleasures of sin for a season;*

He chose rather to suffer affliction with the people of God. He chose a hard life, a lifetime of affliction, rather than enjoy the pleasures of sin for a season. Sin only lasts for a season. He sacrificed for the greater good. He sacrificed it to invest in people that was worth it. You can't celebrate the memory, of Dr. Martin Luther King unless you acknowledge the sacrifice. The sacrifice, as one preacher pointed out so well. A precocious student, he skipped both the ninth and the twelfth grade and entered Morehouse College at age fifteen without formally graduating from high school. In 1948, he graduated from Morehouse with a Bachelor of Arts degree in sociology and enrolled in Crozer Theological Seminary in Chester, Pennsylvania, from which he graduated with a Bachelor of Divinity degree in 1951. Then in 1955, he graduated from Boston University with his Ph.D. in Theology. Although he could've lived in an area far removed from the ills of society and his people, but he chose to live amongst them. Sacrificed the safety of his family.

I don't know if you know already, but baseball is my favorite sport, it took over when the Knicks were doing so badly, but I formed a real healthy liking for baseball. In baseball, there is a particular play called a 'Sac Fly'. Its full name is a sacrifice fly. The batter who is in the box says I'm going to hit a sacrifice fly. I may not get on base but I'm going to hit the ball so that my teammate can make it home so that they can score. I'm going to sacrifice myself so that somebody else could make it home. Perhaps you are reading this, and you realize that you wouldn't be here right now if your mother or father didn't sacrifice themselves so that you could get an education. Some of you wouldn't be here right now if it wasn't for grandma who sacrificed the pleasures of life for the greater good. Aren't you glad that over 2000 years ago Jesus Sacrificed himself for some sinners like us, so that we could make it home.

So, if you gonna celebrate Dr. Martin Luther King day, you just can't celebrate the dream, you gotta celebrate the action. Because last time I checked nobody has ever been killed just for having dreams. I've never read or seen in the news that someone was murdered just for dreaming.

One of my favorite artists says, "You could be a dreamer, but don't live in your bed".

In other words, you gotta wake up at some time and do something.

Shamefully and sadly and we have frozen Dr. King's legacy to a single moment. Next month McDonalds, and every nationally syndicated television network will play the words, "I have a dream one day my four little children will live in a nation where they will not be judged by the color their skin, but by the content of their character." According to Mr. Michael Eric Dyson, we have turned him into a rhetorical ventriloquist. We are using him to speak words that he articulated without the meanings that he intended.

That's why VH1, can run promos of Martin Luther King Jr, and then show Love and Hip Hop NY, Love and Hip Hop Atlanta, Mob Wives, Basketball Wives, Maury Povich can mock and laugh at the plight of the urban family whether it is black or white on a nationally syndicated television show early in the morning. Those shows don't profile or speak for everyone. They are just a microcosm of the real picture, that so easily gets ignored.

Last time I checked schools in urban communities are still inadequately funded, last time I checked inflation continues to increase poor communities. Last time I checked it cost a lot of money to be poor. Last time I checked poor people are still working harder for less money. Paying more for less, paying more for cars, paying more for insurance, more for houses based on discriminatory changes based on color and zip codes. Working longer hours to live shorter lives. Working longer hours only to have what we've earned only to be taken by someone who did nothing to help you get it.

    The question is how far are you willing to go to help somebody? How uncomfortable would you get, to make someone else comfortable? Moses, is still high off of his social progressive movement decides to come back out amongst the people. He notices two Hebrews fighting amongst themselves. Throwing punches, body slamming each other, rolling in the dirt. It's kind of crazy because here is the oppressed, oppressing each other. You would think that they would've had enough of beating and mistreatment from the Egyptians. You would think that they would've come together and put their strength together to help each other instead of breaking each other down.

It hurts me when I hear that when it comes to gun violence in our communities, its at the hands of each other. It's us killing us. When I go to the barbershop in Brooklyn and see the kids fighting. It's us fighting us. When I turn the radio to a local station and all I hear is us dissing us. When I turn on the tv it's us making shows to exploit us. We do more damage to each other, and in some cases we have become the biggest threats to ourselves. We have borrowed the language of the KKK and become co-conspirators to the destruction of our race. Then when a Moses comes up and says, What's wrong with you, why in the world are you hitting and hurting your brother? We then answer back just like Hebrew, "Who died and made you ruler and judge over us? You gonna kill us just like you did with the Egyptian. Do you think you better than us? Do you think you all that? Do you think you the man simply because you all edumacated and stuff?

Listen to me, in some cases whenever you try to help people they will make up and say a whole bunch of wack stuff about you, just to throw you off. It's messed up how after Martin has done all that he could do, that's when they started saying that he plagiarized his Ph.D., he was a womanizer, he didn't write I have a dream, but he heard a little girls prayer, and took the idea and claimed it as his own. It's really messed up how there are folk out there that will try to diminish the good you try to do, by putting a light on some of your mistakes….

One of the prices that you will pay when you help somebody is that you run the risk of being dissed by your own people. You run the risk of being rejected and ostracized from your own community. Doesn't the bible say that He came to his own, and his own received him not. How many times have we read in the word, where Jesus would heal people then they would reject him, once he preached the truth? Isn't that what they did, when Jesus rose up Lazarus from the dead? I mean He raised a man from the dead, no life no breath in his body, nothing, raised him from the dead, and instead of celebrating it they began to plot and scheme to find ways to kill him.

Isn't that what they've done to our former president, as soon as he got in office the first thing that the Cornel Wests, and the Tavis Smileys started saying, that he hasn't done anything for us, he hasn't done anything for anyone but himself. He is president of the united states, not the president of the NAACP. I hear the cries, but I always got to ask myself what in the world have I done for the people that are around me.

But that's not why I do good for other people. I don't do it because I'm expecting you to like me. I'm not doing it because I'm trying to position myself somewhere. I'm doing this because it's right. I'm doing it because the very fibers in my body that God has produced in me tells me that I gotta help somebody.

The word says that when Moses heard the Egyptian say that, he fled to Midian because word had gotten out. His picture was on every milk carton. EMW Egypt's Most Wanted. Have you seen this man? He is wanted for murder in Egypt. His whereabouts are unknown. Please be careful he's probably armed and dangerous. Moses says, this thing that I've done is made known. The word is out, so Moses ran. Look ain't nothing wrong with Moses running, he was scared, and he was not prepared for the task at hand that God was calling him to do. This was just a pre-cursor to the greater calling. But I wanna focus on "this thing is known".

When you do what's right it will be made known, it won't be a secret, but the God of the universe sees it, and he honors it. God kept Moses while he was in Midian. Moses thought he was finished, but for God it was only the beginning. When you do something for others, God will turn around and bless you in the process. Look at what God did, later in the chapter the word tells us that while he was in Midian he saw some women, that were being chased off by some shepherds, but Moses could not be silent, went and helped them out, and watered their sheep. When the girls got back home, they told their daddy what happened, and one of them said an Egyptian man helped us out. Daddy said go get him. When he got him the dad gave his daughter Ziporah to be his wife. God turned around and blessed Moses with a sistah. How do I know she was a sistah? Because when Miriam saw her she spoke out against her, and God cursed her with leprocy. God gave Moses a shorty to ride or die with him. That's why when you do good to others, it will be known. God will bless you with favor. Folks got it messed up thinking that God will only bless you with money. No way! God blesses you with things that the IRS can't tax. With things that you won't see in your paycheck. God gives you peace that passes all understanding. When you do unto others it will be made known.

Okay, I don't know if you have ever noticed but when you use the bathroom in a plane there is often times a little message that says as a courtesy can you please clean up before you leave. Leave it better for somebody else who's coming behind you. Don't leave it a mess, but clean it up as a courtesy. And all I'm trying to say is that for me as a preacher as a courtesy it's my job to leave wherever I am better for the person that is coming behind me. As a courtesy it's up to you leave your position better for the next person that is coming behind you. As a courtesy leave it better for the younger generation that is coming up behind you. As a courtesy preach what you've been taught so that those that are coming up behind you, can do the same for someone else. As a courtesy if you gonna take the bus to get somewhere, send it back so somebody else can take a ride...

Rise up don't be silent
The pugnacious persistence of Malcolm X
The vigor of Marcus Garvey
The willpower of Huey P. Newton
The dedication of Steven Biko
The purpose of the Little Rock Nine
The immobility of Rosa Parks
The balladry of Maya Angelou, Langston Hughes, Nikki Giovanni, Gwendolyn Brooks, Countee Cullen…
The harmonious tones of Marian Anderson, Louis Armstrong, Josephine Baker, Nat King Cole, Duke Ellington, Mahalia Jackson, Billie Holiday,

Rise up with the determination of Martin Luther King Jr.

I wanna close with these words…

Yes, if you want to say that I was a drum major, say that I was a drum major for justice. (*Amen*) Say that I was a drum major for peace. (*Yes*) I was a drum major for righteousness. And all of the other shallow things will not matter. (*Yes*) I won't have any money to leave behind. I won't have the fine and luxurious things of life to leave behind. But I just want to leave a committed life behind. (*Amen*) And that's all I want to say.

If I can help somebody as I pass along,
If I can cheer somebody with a word or song,
If I can show somebody, he's traveling wrong,
Then my living will not be in vain.
If I can do my duty as a Christian ought,
If I can bring salvation to a world once wrought,
If I can spread the message as the master taught,
Then my living will not be in vain.

Reflection

- What are some things in society do you feel compelled about to raise your voice?
- Moses stepped in during an act of injustice, are there moments in your life where you feel like you could have, or should have stepped in during an injustice?
- Some would say that a true sacrifice is giving up something that you love, so that others can be blessed. What can you see yourself sacrificing for the fight against injustice?

PRAYER

Thank you for the voice You have given to me. May I always use it to speak up for those who can't speak for themselves. May my words reflect the relationship that I have with you, and the words of my mouth be pleasing unto you. Thank you for this gift Father.

AMEN

10

Jesus, The Trouble Maker

Matt. 10:34-39

Think not that I am come to send peace on earth: I came not to send peace, but a sword. For I am come to set a man at variance against his father, and the daughter against her mother, and the daughter in law against her mother in law. And a man's foes shall be they of his own household. He that loveth father or mother more than me is not worthy of me: and he that loveth son or daughter more than me is not worthy of me. And he that taketh not his cross, and followeth after me, is not worthy of me. He that findeth his life shall lose it: and he that loseth his life for my sake shall find it.

Eugene Patterson Interpretation

"Don't think I've come to make life cozy. I've come to cut—make a sharp knife-cut between son and father, daughter and mother, bride and mother-in-law—cut through these cozy domestic arrangements and free you for God. Well-meaning family members can be your worst enemies. If you prefer father or mother over me, you don't deserve me. If you prefer son or daughter

over me, you don't deserve me. If you don't go all the way with me, through thick and thin, you don't deserve me. If your first concern is to look after yourself, you'll never find yourself. But if you forget about yourself and look to me, you'll find both yourself and me.

When I was a teenager, I was a mischievous little bandit. I would love to cause trouble at the expense of others. I had no brothers, but I had two older sisters, and they would pick on me from time to time. And because they were seven and eight years older than me, and much more smarter, it was extremely difficult to get revenge on them, so I would just have to take the abuse from day to day. But since I could not get them back, I took my frustration out on other family members that were weaker than me.

I remember my cousin from England was coming to America to spend some time with us, and immediately I started cooking up a master plan. What could I do to make his stay in America a memorable one? Well on the first night I let him enjoy his rest, after all, he was out all day, flying all day for six hours and he needed his rest.

But the second night he was mine. I put shaving cream in his hand while he was sleeping, then I tickled his ear with piece of string and just sat back and watched him smack himself in the face with the shaving cream.

I remember one night pouring a glass of water in his bed while he was sleeping to make it appear that he had done something during the night and when he woke up I was pointing the finger at him saying, "You nasty!

I didn't stop there; I took my talents to school. My friends and I couldn't stand this teacher; it seemed like she was always picking on me. My friends and I could never understand why she would get so angry at us for not doing our homework. Anyway, we knew that she liked to sit down all the time, so we decided to take some Krazy glue and glued her chair to the floor. We sat back and laughed as she struggled to pull the chair out.

I was a little troublemaker, and that was just the half of it. Well, what is a troublemaker. The Webster's Dictionary defines a troublemaker as such, *a person who habitually causes difficulty or problems, esp. by inciting others to defy those in authority.*

It's easy to see me as a troublemaker, and I'm sure that many of you can picture a few troublemakers that you know, but if you will allow me to say this, Jesus was a troublemaker.

Lets look at the text, Jesus says, "Do not think that I came to bring peace on earth. I did not come to bring peace but a sword."

Jesus said if you think that I came to make things cozy and nice then I'm sorry you have misunderstood. You have got things wrong. The problem with the Jews was that they thought Jesus would bring them political peace and material prosperity.

Some Christians have this same mentality. Christians have this idea that serving God all of a sudden peace and prosperity are supposed to come your way, or to fall in your lap. Everything is supposed to go right, just because you are doing right. For some of us, we think that the moment you become a leader everybody is supposed to listen to what you have to say. No! There will be on criticisms. Folk are not going to support you, and every program, and every presentation.

Jesus says, No Way! I came to bring a sword, a sharp sword. The sword that I bring is so sharp that *it will set a man against his father, a daughter against her mother, and a daughter-in-law against her mother-in-law, and a man's' enemies will be those of his own household."* When I show up, I cause trouble because this gospel message that I preach can comfort the afflicted, but it can also afflict those that are too comfortable.

Church, friends, young people, leaders, or whoever is reading this right now expect that when you are true disciples, some people won't like you. Some people would want nothing to do with you. I come to church with the full expectation that there will be some messages that folk will dislike and despise me for. I am not surprised that when I walk into to some places, conversations must come to cessation.

I expect not to be invited to some parties. I expect not to be included in some plans. I expect not be favored by every man and woman. I expect for people to lie on me, I am not surprised when people to whisper about me. I am not surprised when people to walk away from me. I am not surprised when plan to conspire against me.

But what matters to me is that God favored me. God still covers me, and that will not change me

> *I will still walk with probity*
>
> *I will live with integrity.*
>
> *Show my morality.*
>
> *Dress with decency.*
>
> *Love with honesty.*
>
> *Stay in serenity.*
>
> *Speak with authority*
>
> *Keep my dignity*
>
> *Live in humility*
>
> *Until one day I will live in eternity*

Why?!? Because God favors me. I don't need friends and associates who are not committed to extreme discipleship. Jesus says my words will bring division. Your own loved ones will turn their backs on you. This is not the intention of God, but it's just the way things are.

We know that Paul was stoned, Peter was crucified upside down, John was thrown into a caldron of hot burning oil. Martin Luther was excommunicated. They dug up John Wycliffe's bones and burned them. John Huss was burned on a stake. Ellen White was shipped to Australia, that's just to name a few.

Jesus was emphasizing the price of discipleship. Discipleship says that even if I have no family, God is all I need. Even if I have no job, the Father has work for me. Even if I lose all my money, I know that the righteous won't be forsaken nor his seed will be begging for bread.

Today you have been handpicked and selected by God to a higher a service. Today you have been given the honor of being laborers in the vineyard of the Lord.

It is important that you realize that the prosperity of the church does not solely depend upon the pastor, but it falls upon the leaders as well.

As a leader, it is imperative that you realize that there will be times when you will have to endure hardship for the sake of others, but never forget that God is with you every step that you take. God says, *I will instruct thee and teach thee in the way which thou shalt go: I will guide thee with mine eye.* When you feel weak, *He gives power to the weak, And to those who have no might He increases strength."*

When the responsibility of the work appears to be a flood, and when the scorns and criticisms feel like flames all around you...God says, *"When thou passest through the waters, I will be with thee; and through the rivers, they shall not overflow thee: when thou walkest through the fire, thou shalt not be burned; neither shall the flame kindle upon thee."* Press on leader...do the work of the Lord with no apology, no favors, no compromise, and no applause. But do the work because you are sure that God has anointed you and appointed you to serve in the house of the Lord.

Church there is bad trouble, and then there is good trouble.

I'll deal with **bad trouble** first. Bad trouble comes to those that go out looking for trouble. I mean those that pick fights and walk around the place acting big and bad, and when the tables turn on them and folk come looking for you because they want revenge...that is bad trouble.

Bad trouble comes to those that are sneaky and conniving.

Bad trouble comes to those that hand out mortgage loans with high-interest rates and even when they try to come up with 700 billion dollars that's still not enough to get them out of trouble.

Bad troubles comes to bullies...Bad trouble comes to those that reject and revile God. Bad troubles falls upon those that consistently and persistently manipulate people whether that be financially, physically and even spiritually.

Bad trouble will fall upon those that are described in *Matt 25:41...Then shall he say also unto them on the left hand, Depart from me, ye cursed, into everlasting fire, prepared for the devil and his angels:*

Bad trouble is often brought upon us whenever we go outside of the will of God.

But then there is good trouble. What Yes Good trouble?

Look at what Jesus says to those that were in trouble or troubled by a system because they served God.

Jesus stood up on a mountain and pronounced blessings for those that were in trouble...and said

Blessed are the poor in spirit, for theirs is the kingdom of God

Blessed are those who mourn, for they shall be comforted

Blessed are the meek, For they shall inherit the earth

Blessed are those who hunger and thirst for righteousness for they shall be filled

Blessed are the pure in heart, for they shall see God

Blessed are the peacemakers, for they shall be called the Sons of God...

The text says Blessed are the peacemakers, not peacekeepers. Peacekeepers are completely and totally opposite of peacemakers. Peacemakers and peacekeepers have nothing in common in my opinion. I know that they share the same prefix, but the meaning is emphasized on the suffix.

Peacekeepers would do everything possible to keep the peace. They just want to make sure that things stay the way they are, and hope that it does not change into a revolt. Peacekeepers just want to keep the peace. Peacekeepers say that hey as long as things are going the way that they are going now just don't fight...

But a Peacemaker, on the other hand, is totally different. A peacemaker will tell a peacekeeper step aside something needs to be done. A peacemaker will go at all lengths to bring about peace even if that causes some trouble. A peacemaker is willing to relinquish some relationships, be called all sorts of names because they know that it's time for things to change. A peacemaker will look at a system and say, this thing is corrupt. This thing is old and broken.

I wish we had some more spiritual troublemakers. I wish we had some more spiritual troublemaking preachers who aren't afraid to cry aloud and spare not the sinner. To call sin as it is, and preach with conviction.

I wish there were some more young people who would use the power of prayer to shake up this world. The power of speech to speak against injustice

For there was a troublemaker named Martin Luther King Jr., who stood up for some sanitation workers.

It was a troublemaker named Huey P. Newton who read that citizens have the right to bear arms....

It was a troublemaker named Rosa Parks who decided to sit on the front of the bus and not the back

It was a troublemaker named Ellen G. White who got the inspiration of God and wrote what she was told.

But there was a greater troublemaker by the name of Jesus Son of the Living God, who said, "The Spirit of the Lord is upon Me because He hath anointed me to preach the gospel to the poor."

It is the same man who walked into the temple and overturned the tables of the money exchangers and said, "my house shall be called a house of prayer."

It is this same man who picked corn on the Sabbath day and told the Pharisees, "you would rather pick your old donkey out of a ditch than to good on the Sabbath day."

It is this same man who said, "destroy this temple, and in three days I will raise it up."

It is this same man that caused trouble for Ananias and Caphias when he was on trial. They said are you the Christ? Jesus looked at them and said, Thou Hast, Said it! In other words, I don't have to answer you just confessed it. And as a matter of fact, Jesus said you will the Son of Man riding on a cloud when ten thousand upon thousands of angels ready to redeem my servants.

Good trouble comes to those that are in the will of God because Good trouble will have a better outcome...

Jesus says, *"And he who does not take his cross and follow after Me is not worthy of Me"* If you are not willing to go through some things then you are not worthy of me... you don't deserve me.

I wish some of our young brothers and sisters would take that seriously. Jesus says if you are not willing to commit to this relationship then you don't deserve me. Brothers and Sisters if this Negro or Negrette is not willing to commit to you. Is not willing to pray with you. Is not willing to come to church with you. Is not willing to respect you. If they come with a whole bunch of drama, I don't care how cute they are, or how much money they got, or how good they smell. They don't deserve you.

Jesus is saying I did not die on the cross for you to use me whenever you need me. Whenever things are going bad, that's when you are my closest friend. I did not die on the cross for you to be praising me and singing hymns, so on Sunday, you could start acting all brand new. I did not die so that you could have salvation how you want it and when you want it. Jesus says you don't deserve me!

You know what Church it gets better. Jesus says He who finds his life will lose it, and he who loses his life for my sake shall find it.

Trouble Won't Last Always

If you try to find your life in material possessions, or if you try to find your life in friends and having large entourages then that will avail to nothing. So many try to find their life in money, cars, and fame. They tried to find themselves here and establish themselves through education and a job...then you have done nothing but made a place for yourself on this earth.

But Jesus credits those who seek the Kingdom of God first and His righteousness. God says find your identity in me. Secure this first, and I will give you the rest. I will provide. I may not give you as much as others have, but what I have is better than what your family can give you, friends can give you, and even big corporations.

Jesus says your mother may have given you life on earth, but I will give you life in the new earth

Your Father may teach you how to shoot a ball and jump high, but I can give you wings so you can mount up with wings like an eagle

Your brother may be able to defend you when bully's show up, but I can raise up a standard so that the enemy your adversary will not have his way with you.

Your sister may be able to comfort you when you cry, But I can give you the peace that surpasses all human thinking and wisdom.

Jesus says if you lose your life on earth. If you can learn how to deny yourself, pick up your cross and follow me. I promise I will give you something greater in the world to come.

Your trouble here on earth won't always last because the Bible says, "*For in the time of trouble he shall hide me in his pavilion: in the secret of his tabernacle shall he hide me; he shall set me up upon a rock.*

Psalm 50:15 says, *"Call upon me in the day of trouble, and I will deliver you, and you shall glorify me.*

God is our refuge and strength, a very present help in the time of trouble

Though I walk in the midst of trouble. You will revive me; You will stretch out Your hand against the wrath of my enemies. And your right hand will save me.

For it was God that parted the Red Sea for the Israelites, so they can cross over.

For it was God that won the battle for King Jehosophat when the armies came in to take his life.

It was God that cooled the burning furnace for the three Hebrew boys and saved them in the fire.

It was God who shut the mouths of the lions when Daniel was in the den.

It was Jesus who came to earth to die for some sinners that were in trouble. Sin demanded that every man should die, but Jesus stretched out his hands died on Calvary and rose up early Sunday Morning with all power and strength in His hands.

Trouble won't last always. You won't always cry every night. You won't always be living from check to check. You won't have to worry about where you are going to sleep tomorrow. You won't have to worry about terrorism. You won't have to worry about those that ridicule you, young people..those that make fun of you because you don't curse, fight, smoke or drink.

Trouble Won't Last Always

Run with perseverance. Run with endurance. Know this leader that we are in troubling times, the economy is collapsing. Oppression still exists, and racism is alive. There is genocide in certain places of Africa, terrorism in the Middle East and Israel insists on dropping bombs on Palestine. Pesky political leaders still impose their machinations to rule and dominate the poor, people can be bought and sold, but not your leader, you must stand for the right.

For if you don't stand up the church will be debilitated

The community will be devastated

The people will be dominated

The world will be disintegrated

The children will be truncated

The race will be apocopated and eviscerated

Plan your programs with an apocalyptic theme, for we are in the last days. Not these limp wrist programs, we don't need to play games. We don't need to see more skits about nothing; We don't need to have more concerts with people singing other people's songs. If you do anything, sing with a purpose, teach with a purpose, preach with a purpose, love with a purpose, but above all those things live for a purpose in Jesus.

For Jesus was a troublemaker…..

Reflection

- What do you think about the idea that Jesus was a troublemaker?
- What is the difference between a peacemaker and peacekeeper? When do you think it's right to cause a little trouble, in order to make peace?
- When you think about all the trouble in this world, a lot of people would say we don't need to do anything but to wait on Jesus because when He comes back, all of this will be taken care of. Do you agree, or disagree with that statement and why?

PRAYER

Father, I thank you for all that you have done for me. Please allow me to be the agent of change that you need in this world. May you please give me the courage to be bold for You, so that Your name will be glorified in all the earth.

AMEN

11

With Liberty and Justice, for Just Us

Jeremiah 33:14-16
The days are surely coming, says the Lord, when I will fulfill the promise I made to the house of Israel and the house of Judah. In those days and at that time I will cause a righteous Branch to spring up for David; and he shall execute justice and righteousness in the land. In those days Judah will be saved and Jerusalem will live in safety. And this is the name by which it will be called: "The Lord is our righteousness."

(This sermon was preached a few days before July 4, 2017)

Just a few days from today, families will gather together for a celebration. The grill will be fired up, potato salad will be served, sweet tea will be liberally poured out, and the barbecue sauce will drip ever so slowly off of the beef ribs. If you have a kind host he will ensure that the griller isn't overlooked or over cooked. Why you ask because this is Independence Day. The day of honoring those that have fought freedom, and those that we have lost in the battle. We celebrate and rejoice the victory over the British, for the ramparts we watched were so gallantly streaming, and the rockets' red glare the bombs bursting in air, gave proof through the night that our flag was still there. We sing of freedom, peace, liberty, and happiness, but yet still this dream and hope is not felt by all. As America celebrates its freedom, we must also acknowledge it's unfreedom. One hand we proudly raise up the Stars and Stripes but cover up the scars and stripes that have been left on the backs of slaves. On one hand, we will lift up the Statue of Liberty and those poetic words "Give me your tired, your poor, your huddled masses, yearning to breathe free, but on the other hand, we are making deals to marginalized the Mexican, and vilify the Muslim. With one hand we will pay tribute to all the slain officers that have lost their lives which we should, but on the other hand we will not acknowledge or hold a tribute for all the people who have lost their lives at the hand of the police, instead we will continue to add more people to the Black Dead Parents Club.

That's why Big Sean said, "Slavemaster take our names, 5-0 take the shot, young souls take the blame, but they can't take away the light."

Sean is simply saying is that the police can take the shot, but yet still the victim can take the blame. Isn't that what we witnessed on the weekend of Father's Day as the jury shamefully, and sagaciously failed to indict the officer that shot Philando in cold-blooded murder in front of his girlfriend and a child? The support of a narrative that somehow he deserved to die. A system that was rooted in the slave watch, of hunting black people down. A system that we all know that there have been multiple reports of white supremacists infiltrating law enforcement to push their racist agenda. Lets we forget Bull Connor who was a cop that hated black people. We don't just have bad cops; we got a bad system. It's crazy that the officer is not guilty, but yet the family receives a 3-million-dollar settlement, just goes to show how willing America is to pay for White Supremacy. With our right hands we say, One nation under God, with liberty and justice for all, but with the left, we make deals with the devil, while we ignore the weak. Naked and you closed shelters, hungry and you cut welfare, I was sick, and you are trying to repeal health care and give big breaks to the wealthy, I was in prison, and instead of visiting me you are in cahoots with the courts, the prisons, and the bail bonds. That's why I was honored to write an op-ed for the Dallas Morning News calling out our DA Faith Johnson for not enacting bail reform as Dallas charges poor people for their freedom and in most cases individuals who are not guilty of their charge. This isn't liberty and Justice for All; this is liberty and justice for Just Them!

Which leads me to the text. Our boy Jeremiah the weeping prophet is a young man who has to speak out against a system that was downright criminal. Verse 1-2 of the chapter starts like this. The word of the Lord came unto Jeremiah a second time while he was in prison...Notice that the text says that the word of the

Lord came to him a second time, which means that he's been in prison for while. Locked up without a trial, I mean who knows why he is still in prison perhaps he had a state-appointed lawyer who could care less about him. Perhaps the judge set the bail too high, and he must now wait in prison until trial. We don't know all of the circumstances, but we do know that he's in incarcerated. His only crime is standing is following God and speaking out against the government.

You do know that their are a whole lot of people out there who will dislike you just because you got a backbone. You do know their got a whole lot of people that will hate you cuz they can't buy you. You know whole lot of people who ain't got nothing going on will hate you cuz you got it going on. Simply because you don't do what they want you to do, so what they do, they will define you and try to confine you.

My favorite preacher always shares this story about a grasshopper. You do know that a grasshopper can jump up to 90 feet. But if you catch it and put inside of a jar to live the grasshopper will jump and keep hitting the ceiling when you take the grasshopper out, he will not jump 90 feet anymore, but instead, it alters it's jumping because it thinks that it's still going to hit the top. I guess what I'm trying to say is that even though it is free, it still acts and behave like it is in a prison. Have you ever noticed that there are people who are prisoners, but they are not in prison? Yeah, you got some folks who have been locked up because they have subjected themselves to the thoughts and ideas of people who love control. Isn't it funny how the people that know the least about you, always have the most to say?

Whenever you live down to other people's standards, you will never be able to live up to God's expectations. I've lived long enough, and learned enough that I can't let people control me, because at the end of the day, you don't have a heaven or hell to put me in. Your job didn't wake me up this morning, your car didn't bring me to the altar. Your degrees did not heal me. Your money didn't purchase my ransom. But it was blood of Jesus! When I thought I lost it all it was God's favor that gave me a new life. So before you judge me, my past, or my character, how about you walk in my shoes, walk the path I traveled, live my sorrow, take my doubts, my fears, my pain, and my laughter. When you lived my life, then you can judge me, but until then get out of my way, my face, and stay in your place, because I got a praise inside of me, that needs to get out, and I can't afford to have no rocks crying out for me.

Prison is a terrible feeling to be free and live like a prisoner. Life on earth can make you feel like you are a prisoner. Laws and policies can leave you feeling like a prisoner. Having no job, can make you feel like a prisoner. No source of income can make you feel like you are prisoner. Prison can make you feel like you are in a lonely dark place. Isolated and abandoned. Trapped, handcuffed, and helpless. Feeling bound can make you want to completely give up. Throw in the towel, walk out of church, and let go of life. But hold on don't leave me yet, but I don't know if you saw this important part of the text.

As I'm reading the text, there are four words that jump out to me that keep saying Pastor Jaime please preach me. Those four words are "The Word of the Lord". There is nothing like the word of the lord, notice when it came unto him while he was in prison. Ain't good to know that the every now and then, that God's word comes in those dark moments. It wasn't until everybody I knew left me, that I heard the word of the Lord. Not when the sun is shining, but I've seen God show up in the night situations of my life. Because, I got all these dark nights, pain and heartache in my life. Because confusion and problems are coming upon me, that should tell me that I must be extremely close to my destiny, to my victory to my breakthrough.

I need a word when I don't know which way to go. I need a word from you Lord. Drown out the noise and let me hear your voice. I need to stand still and know that you are Lord. I need a word. I need a Greater is he that is in me, that he that is in the world. I need a no weapon formed against me shall prosper. I need a word, Lord, in the midst of all of this confusion and I'm facing, I need a trust in the Lord with all your heard and lean not to your own understanding. That's why I'm here today pastor, I need a word, because this prison got me feeling like I should quit. I need to tell whoever is reading this right now, strength doesn't come without a struggle. You can't have a testimony without a test. Muscles are developed when the weight is on you.

If you're from the old school and you use film, you know a thing or two that pictures are developed in the light, but they gotta go through something in the dark. The photographer knows that you gotta shake that thing and leave it in the dark for a little while, but he pulls it out at the appointed time. Is there a witness in here today, that I'm in the dark, but I know God's got his hands on me. I know that he's developing me, for a greater purpose.

The word of God says, "The day will come..." I like that; the Message Bible says, "Watch this! It's coming!

I'm gonna keep my promise. Please remember that Israel and Judah are in a turbulent and terrible predicament. The gov't has a king that likes to tweet, excuse me put out decrees that sets the entire nation back. God tells them watch this, Ok the Hebrew is telling me that it's giving off the image of looking ahead instead of what's around you. It's like looking at a picture that is totally different from what is going on around you.

Let me try to paint this picture. There was some turbulence on a flight. The pilot told the passengers to stay seated and put on their seatbelts because the flight was going to get rough. There was on particular gentleman that was sitting next to a little boy who kept smiling. The man next to him asked him why are you smiling, this plane can go down any minute. The little boy said my daddy gave me this picture to look at whenever things get rough. You see this is the house I'm moving too, and he promised me that this will be my room. And sir if you knew my Daddy, then you know that he always keeps his promises.

May I preach to someone in here today. I just need one person who knows that God always has a plan prepared for you, and you know that your Father always keeps his promises. Just don't let what's around you get inside you, that it changes you and makes you put down picture. My point is that the God you serve will always give you previews of coming attractions.

Israel just waits, it's coming. Hold on Israel and Judah. Be patient; I will keep my promise. I will fulfill my word. I will establish my rulership. I am still in charge. I am still on the throne. I am still God and God all by myself. I am still the creator of this world. I am still he who can speak, and it exists, think and it appears, blink, and it will move. I still hold your hope in the palm of my hands, and I will not let it go. For I know the thoughts that I think towards you, thoughts of peace, and to prosper you and give you an expected end. In other words, I will give you something to believe in.

The text says, "Behold my days are coming when I will keep the promise. In those days and at that time.

Isn't that beautiful? It's that just remarkable. God is saying, that I remember, and have seen what has been done to you, and because you have dealt with plenty, I will do this for you. It almost as if the pain you go through is setting you up for something great. I see the turmoil that you face in this world. I see the calamity and pressure. I witness the injustice, and that's why I will do this.

The word says I will cause a branch of righteousness to grow up onto David. Whenever the Bible refers to branch it is always in reference to something that has been dead, because a new branch will signify new grow.

New Grow.

Every sister reading this book should be shouting right now. You know what new grow is. New grow is unaltered hair that grows naturally from a sisters scalp. When you have chemically-altered ethnic hair, or transitioning hair, new growth is noticed. It's thicker, with greater structure. It is a wonderful and beautiful thing when a sister looks in the mirror and sees new growth. You begin to think about all the wonderful possibilities you can do when you have about an inch of new growth. Because that new growth basically says that something new is happening.

God is saying Hold on Israel. I got New Grow for you. In the midst of lazy and relaxed leadership I will spring up a new branch from what was dead. God is the only person that I know who can bring something out of nothing. How in the world do you create life from out of what is dead? Only God can do it. God has a way of turning things around. God has a wonderful way of flipping things. God has a way of taking the weak and making it strong.

Since we on the topic of hair, I think I oughta go there. Do you remember that old man Bill O'Reilly came after Maxine Waters? He tried to diss that beautiful black hair on her head. He tried to play that sister. He said she looked like she had on a James Brown wig. Now Maxine never did anything to Bill, but Bill felt like he had to go after her. Now I don't know about you but I remember growing up what those old mothers used to say, those old mothers used to say, what are you doing here, I didn't send for you. "Don't Come For me, If I didn't Send for you. Well Bill messed with the wrong sister. After he came for her, Maxine said you need to keep my name out your mouth we all know about you like to harass women. Well some other women heard that and started coming out against Bill O'Reilly and check this out. Maxine Waters still got her job, and Bill has been fired. I know I serve a God that knows how to turn things around. Be careful what you do to God's people, because God has a wonderful way of humbling you. Don't come for me, if I didn't send you!

God says in the midst of this tragic, and terrible leadership. In the midst of this awful rulership, I know that you haven't had a good king since David. I know there is some craziness going on. I know that there is a tweeting, tyrant of a five-year-old on the throne. I know that the leader that you once had who did such a phenomenal job. That leader who always acted like a leader when folk were trying to pull him down. That leader who spoke so eloquently and stood so astute is gone. The leadership has shifted, and God knows that it has been rough in here since 11-9, which was 9-11 for black America. God knows that things aren't the same, so God says I'm going to bring a branch out of dead stump.

Have you ever heard of the Grow Fox or Grow Owl? In case you haven't, it's a toy. My family and I picked up in the bargain bin at toys r us. Apparently they weren't very popular, so they were selling it for a dollar. Since people didn't enjoy it by buying it, they figured that they would throw it to the side. Well, we saw it in the bargain bin, and picked it up, and brought it home. Now what you gotta understand that it's called grow fox and grow owl. We opened the box, and it was just a tree stump. So, we did as the instructions said, submerge it water and leave it there. We left the stump would you know that the next morning when we looked at it, it was still the same, on the second day we looked at it, and it was still the same, but on the third day when we looked at it, something began to happen. It cracked and when it cracked something bigger, beautiful, and different came out of it.

I wish I had a church in here today, the branch that God is referring to is our Savior, Lord, and King. It is about heaven's hero, earths emancipator, the HNIC, head Nazarene in charge. It's a prophetic word. It is look to the future word. It's a word that reminds us of a king who came and died and on the third day rose up with all power in his hands. God says he is the righteous judge. What did this King do? This King stood up in a temple and said that the spirit of the Lord is upon because he hath anointed to me to heal the brokenhearted, preach deliverance to the captives, set at free the oppressed, comfort the brokenhearted and preach the acceptable year of the Lord. What did this king do? This king walked this earth and healed people. What did this king do? This king walked on water, healed a woman with an issue of blood, gave the blind sight, healed a sick girl, restored a withered hand, cleaned some lepers, rode a donkey, fed 5,000 people, calmed a storm, gave a paralytic legs, prayed in a garden, died on a hill, slept in a borrowed tomb, rose up early Sunday morning with all power and might in his hands, and he's still moving today. He's in the midst of the seven candlesticks; he's seated on his throne interceding on our behalf, he's still making a way out of no way. He's still saving lives, putting families back together, restoring the breach that was broken. He still moving, and he's watching, because the text says that he shall execute judgment and righteousness in the land.

Verse sixteen says, "that Judah shall be saved, and Jerusalem shall dwell safely." Can I say this word? You can't do wrong to right people. You can do evil to God's people and get away with it. You can quote me, and live another way. Lets stop saying that people will lose their health insurance, the right language is they will take away your health insurance. You can't talk about my creation like that. You can't do that on God's watch. You can't just ignore your years of heartache and pain that you have done to the Native American, the African American, the Chinese American, the Muslim American, the Latin American. You can't do that. Because God said, I will send a righteous Judge who will administer equality and fairness with Liberty and justice for all. But I gotta be patient. I better learn how to wait.

If you don't mind on this day of independence, I must look to the one that is greater than all this suffering. If you are comfortable with it, then I ask you to say this pledge with me out loud.

I pledge allegiance to the Lamb
With all my strength, with all I am
I will seek to honor his commands
I pledge allegiance to the lamb
to the Lamb of God who bore my pain
who took my place, who wore my shame
I will seek to honor His commands
I pledge allegiance to the Lamb

Reflection

- Do you at times feel like that there are two justice systems in America?
- We all have various expectations of our friends, families, and elected leaders, and the same goes for ourselves. Do you at times find yourself living down to people's expectations or living up to God's expectations for your life?
- God already has a plan ordained for your life. What steps can you take today to begin walking in the path that has already been prepared for you?

PRAYER

Lord, today I ask you to come into me so that your light will shine wherever You want me to be. I know that you are a God that loves justice, fairness, and equality for all of your creation. Please use me to accomplish your will on this Earth, and build your Kingdom.

AMEN

About the Author

Jaime M. Kowlessar is an emerging activist in the Dallas, TX area. He's widely sought-after speaker and facilitator in the area of social justice and political activism. He's travelled to various places equipping and educating people on the need for justice and equality.

www.ingramcontent.com/pod-product-compliance
Lightning Source LLC
Chambersburg PA
CBHW052055110526
44591CB00013B/2217